MICROCOSM · PUBLISHING

MICROCOSM PUBLISHING is Portland's most diversified publishing house and distributor with a focus on the colorful, authentic, and empowering. Our books and zines have put your power in your hands since 1996, equipping readers to make positive changes in their lives and in the world around them. Microcosm emphasizes skill-building, showing hidden histories, and fostering creativity through challenging conventional publishing wisdom with books and bookettes about DIY skills, food, bicycling, gender, self-care, and social justice. What was once a distro and record label was started by Joe Biel in his bedroom and has become among the oldest independent publishing houses in Portland, OR. We are a politically moderate, centrist publisher in a world that has inched to the right for the past 80 years.

Global labor conditions are bad, and our roots in industrial Cleveland in the 70s and 80s made us appreciate the need to treat workers right. Therefore, our books are MADE IN THE USA.

Also by Eleanor C. Whitney:

Quit Your Day Job: Building the DIY Project, Life, and Business of Your Dreams

Quit Your Day Job Workbook: Building the DIY Project, Life, and Business of Your Dreams

RIOT WOMAN

Using Feminist Values to
Destroy the Patriarchy

ELEANOR C. WHITNEY

MICROCOSM PUBLISHING
Portland, Ore

RIOT WOMAN
Using Feminist Values to Destroy the Patriarchy

To join the ranks of high-class stores that feature Microcosm titles, talk to your local rep: In the U.S. COMO (Atlantic), FUJII (Midwest), BOOK TRAVELERS WEST (Pacific), TURNAROUND (Europe), UTP/MANDA (Canada), NEW SOUTH (Australia/New Zealand), GPS in Asia, Africa, India, South America, and other countries, or FAIRE in the gift trade.

For a catalog, write or visit:
Microcosm Publishing
2752 N Williams Ave.
Portland, OR 97227
https://microcosm.pub/RiotWoman

Some names and identifying details have been changed in this book.

Did you know that you can buy our books directly from us at sliding scale rates? Support a small, independent publisher and pay less than Amazon's price at www.Microcosm.Pub

Library of Congress Cataloging-in-Publication Data

Names: Whitney, Eleanor C., author.
Title: Riot woman : using feminist values to destroy the patriarchy / Eleanor C. Whitney.
Description: Portland : Microcosm Publishing, 2021. | Includes bibliographical references. | Summary: "Growing up immersed in the feminist, DIY values of punk, Riot Grrrl, and zine culture of the 1990s and early 2000s gave Eleanor Whitney, like so many other young people who gravitate towards activism and musical subcultures, a sense of power, confidence, community, and social responsibility. As she grew into adulthood she struggled to stay true to those values, and with the gaps left by her punk rock education. This insightful, deeply personal history of early-2000s subcultures lovingly explores the difficulty of applying radical feminist values to real-life dilemmas, and embrace an evolving political and personal consciousness. Whitney traces the sometimes painful clash between her feminist values and everyday, adult realities - and anyone who has worked to integrate their political ideals into their daily life will resonate with the histories and analysis on these pages, such as engaging in anti-domestic violence advocacy while feeling trapped in an unhealthy relationship, envisioning a unified "girl utopia" while lacking racial consciousness, or espousing body positivity while feeling ambivalent towards one's own body. Throughout the book, the words and power of Bikini Kill and other Riot Grrrl bands ground the story and analysis, bringing it back to the raw emotions and experiences that gave this movement its lasting power while offering a complex, contemporary look at the promises and pitfalls of Riot Grrrl-informed feminism"-- Provided by publisher.
Identifiers: LCCN 2021019766 | ISBN 9781648410376 (trade paperback)
Subjects: LCSH: Riot grrrl movement. | Feminism and music.
Classification: LCC ML82 .W5 2021 | DDC 781.64082--dc23
LC record available at https://lccn.loc.gov/2021019766

To all my penpals, zine kids, and Riot Grrrls: I am humbled by the way your words and lives have continued to shape me. For Elissa Nelson, Jordana Swan, and Matt Yu thank you for sharing your visions of creativity and justice with me, even if our time together was too short.

CONTENTS

INTRODUCTION

I was twelve years old the first and last time I uttered the words, "I'm not a feminist, but…"

As soon as they left my mouth I felt a sense of betrayal. If I was for girls and women taking power and being equal, why, exactly, would I not be a feminist? Since that moment I have never questioned whether or not I was a feminist or whether or not feminism was relevant to me. I have, however, continuously questioned what kind of feminism I want to practice and critically examined from where I draw feminist inspiration and guidance.

In high school, when I encountered the writing of bell hooks, the ferocious energy of punk and Riot Grrrl, and the nuanced, intersectional exploration of identity captured in young women's zine writing in the 1990s and early 2000s, I saw clearly the kind of feminist I aspired to be and the type of feminism I strove to practice. Riot Grrrl, the punk feminist movement that generated in Olympia, Washington and Washington DC in the early 1990s took a do-it-yourself, direct approach to feminism: starting bands, organizing conferences, publishing zines, and proclaiming, "The revolution starts here and now within each one of us."[1] I learned quickly that I had to be an intersectional feminist, thinking about how gender, race, class, and sexuality intertwine, and an ally to those who had less societal power and privilege than me. If I was a feminist who stood against oppression and for social justice, my practice and beliefs must be expansive and committed to the liberation of all as opposed to the triumphs of specific women.

---

1 Kathleen Hanna, flyer, 1990, in *The Riot Grrrl Collection*, Lisa Darms, ed. New York: The Feminist Press, 2013, 19.

As an adult, I began this collection of essays because the ascension of a form of mainstream, neo-liberal feminism seemed to be inevitable and like it would keep oppressive structures of power intact under the guise of "feminist empowerment." This type of neoliberal feminism is dangerous because it celebrates and benefits women as disconnected individuals and holds those who rise to the top in business, politics, or the cultural industry as examples of willpower, perseverance, and success for the rest of us. This form of feminism does not look deeply at the structural inequalities that form the foundation of American culture, policy, and our relationship and family structures. It instead centers on individual women's stories of success, downplays how different women have differing access to opportunity and support due to structural oppression, and presents a bland narrative of celebrating women for the sake of being women. Its guises and different flavors include corporate feminism, pop culture feminism, girl power, and white feminism. Overall, these individualized, neo-liberal approaches to feminism ignore how policies that benefit *some* women, often those with privilege, may negatively affect, or be irrelevant to, those coming from communities of color, working class backgrounds, or the LGBTQIA community. In beginning to write the essays in this book I wanted to write a counter narrative, and to celebrate, investigate, and invite readers to practice an intersectional feminism that focuses on liberation for all, not the ascension of a few.

In this cultural moment where mainstream feminism seemed to be merging with mainstream culture, I wondered if the scrappy, Riot Grrrl-influenced feminism that had been dear to me as a teenager, and influenced my adult feminist stance, was still relevant. Despite the fact I that loved the stylish options of feminist t-shirts available to me thanks to feminism's new-found cool, I wanted to have deeper conversations about what it means to enact feminism that went beyond catchy slogans and "personal responsibility" for your corporate career. I wanted to parse Riot Grrrl and the cultural context of the late 1990s and find where those feminist ideals needed to evolve and where they were still relevent and could serve us presently to deepen our commitment to radicalism and liberation for all.

In writing this book I posed a question to myself, which I also pose to you as a reader: how have our feminist practices, beliefs, and ideals grown and changed as we have, and what does it mean to *be* a feminist at this moment in our lives?

At first, I wanted to find a road map for living, and building, a feminist life oriented towards social justice and grounded in my lived reality. What I realized in writing, which should have been obvious, is that there is no map, but there is our collective experience, and when we share that our paths become clearer. These essays document and reflect upon how Riot Grrrl-influenced feminism has influenced my life and a greater feminist discourse in general. I explore how I have worked to live with, stick to, and evolve my principles and identity as a traditionally educated, middle class, white feminist who practices intersectional thinking, and looked critically at how broader cultural movements and trends have shaped feminism more generally. My aim is to encourage readers to embrace a commuity-oreiented feminist life in all its messiness, contradictions, and imperfections using Riot Grrrl as a touch point and illustration of a concentrated expression of radical feminist ideals. Our society is still deeply sexist, racist, homophobic, transphobic, and class-based. Feminism does not wipe away those ingrained beliefs, behaviors and attitudes, which manifest themselves in both small and large ways in our lives and society, but it can give us tools to critique, organize against, and work to move past them.

With the election of Donald Trump, misogyny, racism, and homo- and transphobia that had been here all along moved even more violently into the mainstream eye. Yet this context inspired a surge of organized resistance, much of it led by women of color. This was heavily influenced by Black Lives Matter, movements to end sexual assault on college campuses (and more broadly through #MeToo), and the consistent, grassroots organizing that's been driven by immigrants, the working class, and people of color for decades. During the pandemic in 2020, this organizing took the shape of mutual aid networks, which sprung up across the United States, fulfilling a role in supporting and sustaining many communities that traditional charities or social services could or would not. The Black Lives Matter movement surged into the mainstream, pushing questions about policing, prisons, power, and the violence of whiteness front and center. These movements have positioned intersectionality at their core, and have been an acute source of hope, inspiration, and motivation for me and many others engaged in the active practice of feminism.

The events of 2020 and the early months of 2021, including the pandemic, widespread protest over racial injustice, and an attempted coup by white supremacist followers of Donald Trump, represent a turning point for American culture in terms of where we place value and whose lives are considered as "mattering" on a political, social, and cultural scale. As the world continues to shift and the project of recognizing and addressing inequity on a local and global scale becomes increasingly urgent, those of us who practice feminism need to share our stories of coming to consciousness, and how we live and practically act on that consciousness, in order to build power and sustain our movements for justice. Some of us here are new, and some of us have been thinking, writing, organizing, and living as feminists for a long time, and we all need to listen to and support each other to move forward as a culture.

I profoundly believe that an intersectional, social justice oriented, grassroots feminism has space for all who see equality and social justice as core to our collective survival. That sharing, owning, and taking of responsibility for who and where we are will help move us forward.

This book is my feminist process laid bare, and my contribution to an ongoing dialogue of how feminism has and can continue to shape who we are and how we decide to act in the world.

PART ONE

....

FEMINIST COMING OF AGE

THE RADICAL POTENTIAL OF RIOT GRRRL

"Women in rock!" trumpeted the headline of a rumpled *Spin* magazine on the coffee table. It was a cold, grey, April day in Maine, and I sat on an overstuffed couch of a recording studio waiting to record my clarinet part. Around me other members of my high school jazz band shifted quietly, humming their solos to themselves or idly flipping through back issues of *Rolling Stone*. I slid the copy of *Spin*, an arbiter of 1990s alternative culture cool, across the table, feigning casual interest, and started rifling through the pages.

"Inside the Riot Grrrl Revolution!" belted another headline, and I felt a shock of instant connection as my eyes slid across photos of girls my age in Olympia, Washington, trotting through a crosswalk in colorful knee socks, tight thrift store t-shirts and short skirts, hair bedecked in plastic barrettes. According to the article, these girls were playing in bands, putting out records, organizing music festivals, and hosting "Riot Grrrl" meetings to talk about their lives. The need to join stabbed me like a sharp pain in my side. I covertly slipped the magazine into my bag.

The movement known as Riot Grrrl began in the early 1990s, loosely centered in Olympia, Washington and Washington DC. These cities, and rock scenes, had also helped nurture bands like Nirvana, who found popular success, but Riot Grrrl remained purposely underground and independent. It coalesced around majority-women punk bands like Bikini Kill and Bratmobile, was championed by independent record labels like Kill Rock Stars, K

Records, and Chainsaw Records, and made up of a loose network of young women. These girls used their bands, self-published magazines called zines, and meetings, shows, and conferences they organized to speak up about sexism and injustice in society and their personal lives. They also participated in organizng and protests, especially around reproductive rights, abortion access, and against sexual violence. The music was immediate and brash and the lyrics were often politically confrontational and deeply personal.

With their flamboyant style that appropriated little girls' t-shirts and hair accessories, combined with an insistence on centering the voices and experiences of young women, the mainstream media, including outlets like *Newsweek, USA Today,* and the *Washington Post,* seized on Riot Grrrl as a cultural phenomenon. This served to both open it to a wider audience and caused rifts between some of the early participants about the definition and direction of Riot Grrrl. Despite continued coverage by underground-attuned but mainstream press outlets like *Spin* and *Sassy* magazines, by this time in the mid-1990s most mainstream press dubbed Riot Grrrl passe. The acute, feminist anger that had driven bands like Bikini Kill to notoriety was being commercially smoothed out into vague notions, sexualized "girl power." This shift was embodied by manufactured pop groups like the Spice Girls or a folk and piano inflected gentleness favored by Canadian singer-songwriter Sarah McLachlan, one of the organizers of the women-centered music festival Lilith Fair. Riot Grrrl was all new to me, however, and I was elated to discover that there were other girls who had the audacity to revel in the anger they felt at injustice in society, especially around sexism, racism, and homophobia, and the difference they felt from their peers.

The next Sunday I met my boyfriend, Link, and our friends, a mixture of theatre kids and bookish, awkward loners, for our tradition of combing endlessly through bargain bins of used albums at Bullmoose Music, a basement that smelled like a mixture of dusty vinyl, mildew, patchouli incense, and pizza from the restaurant next door. That afternoon I knew exactly what I was looking for. I had made a list of bands described as "Riot Grrrl classics" in the article and I quickly grabbed CDs by Beat Happening, Bikini Kill, Elliott Smith (a male favorite of the Riot Grrrls, the *Spin* journalist had explained), and Sleater-Kinney as if there was a crowd behind me who had been secretly waiting until just this moment to snatch them up before me. I hoped that by possessing the music of this movement I could begin to feel a part of it. I didn't know how to find other girls who liked punk or Riot Grrrl or if they even existed in Southern Maine at the time, and while I had heard there were internet forums on America Online where you could meet other feminists, I didn't really know how to find them. The used CDs were my best hope for now.

"Hm," sniffed Link, shrugging his shoulders while reviewing my purchases over a post-record store slice of pizza, "None of these bands ever signed to a major label. This movement is really just a footnote to grunge and Alternative."

Link's attitude reflected the prevailing, pop culture notion that Riot Grrrl was passe. During the early-to-mid 1990s grunge craze, when major labels were scouring cities like Seattle for the next big band, these labels routinely courted bands like Bikini Kill.

Lead singer Kathleen Hanna admits she asked labels to send CDs of their other artists to check them out, only to sell them for rent money. Ultimately, the band decided not to sign to a major label in order to pursue a vision of creating a "feminist youth culture that was participatory and would change society," according to drummer Tobi Vail.[2]

That night I dropped Sleater-Kinney's "Call the Doctor" into my CD player and pushed the play button, my fingers shaking. I was anxious as to whether or not I would like it. It was really important that I liked it.

> "They want to socialize you / They want to purify you / They want to dignify and analyze and terrorize you…"

It blasted out of my speakers like a missive from an alien world. The detuned tone of the guitars and the warbling, searing vocals were almost frightening. The brief songs were full of distorted guitars and barely contained rage. They loudly defied the quiet perfection that young women were supposed to be and achieve. It felt like coming home.

There was an urgency to the women's voices that was unlike other, safer "women in rock" Link had included on mixed tapes for me, like Liz Phair, PJ Harvey, or Juliana Hatfield. Those musicians had a feminist flavor to their lyrics, but weren't necessarily overtly political and, by virtue of writing more pop-friendly songs and working with major labels and mainstream producers, some of their work had a more radio-friendly appeal. Listening to bands like Sleater-Kinney and Bikini Kill gave me the sense that it was

2 Sara Marcus, *Girls to the Front*, New York: Harper Perennial, 2010, 272.

possible to express oneself as a girl and command your listeners' attention without being smoothed out or heavily produced. Their songs reached down and pulled at all the raw anger and unfocused determination that was coursing through me. Their songs harnessed my tempestuous emotions, concentrated them, and burned into me like a cannonball.

Similar to Tobi Vail's hope that Bikini Kill fans would become part of a participatory youth culture, listening to Riot Grrrl bands made me feel not only like I had to learn how to make music like this, but that it was within my power to do so. Learning guitar and being in a rock band became a feminist act. As Riot Grrrl came out of the punk movement in general, there was a prevailing attitude of "DIY," or "do it yourself"—that anyone could play in bands, put on shows, form their own labels, and generally create their own "scene." Coming from a rural area, the immediacy of DIY was incredibly appealing and I thought playing guitar was my key to participation in Riot Grrrl culture, though I wasn't really sure how.

Despite the relative popularity of women in rock bands in the 1990s, playing electric guitar was still perceived as the purview of boys. Venturing to the guitar shop to buy my first electric guitar with money I earned from mowing neighbors' lawns felt like stepping into hostile, masculine territory. Men who were fans of grunge and independent rock in the 1990s were often perceived as more sensitive and evolved from macho ideas of masculinity, with their long, flowing hair, and men like Kurt Cobain, Pearl Jam's Eddie Vedder, and Sonic Youth's Thurston Moore, who were often outspoken about feminist politics, were perceived as role models. However, many teenage boys were attracted to these bands because of the angsty lyrics and thrashing guitars, and did not necessarily develop an analysis of how sexism and masculinity shaped their lives and their perceptions of and behaviors towards women.

In the mid-to-late 1990s, the concept of "girl power" as popularized by manufactured pop group the Spice Girls permeated the media. Nike ran a series of ad campaigns with the tagline "if you let me play" touting the strength of girls and the benefits of encouraging their participation in sports. Women-run skatewear company Poot! released a popular series of t-shirts declaring "Girls Kick Ass," which was sported widely by girls beyond the skater community. Despite these feminist-leaning slogans, the overall cultural message young women still received was that finding a boyfriend (but not getting pregnant) was of paramount importance. However, as young women learned to assert themselves, there was not readily accessible information about how to navigate the backlash that might come with their power. There was also a lack of open conversation about how power and gendered expectations could translate into abuse in a young relationship.

While awareness of the impact of bullying, sexism, and power has grown thanks to ongoing organizing and activism over the past few decades, especially post-#metoo, the organization loveisrespect notes that nearly 1.5 million high school students nationwide experience physical abuse from a dating partner in a single year, a figure that exceeds the rates of other types of youth violence. The movement against sexual assault that was nurtured and grew on college campuses in the mid-2010s helped open the conversation around sex and consent, but in 2018 only 8 states required sex education classes to mention consent by law.[3] Even President Bill Clinton's landmark Violence Against Women Act, first passed in 1994 (which provided funding for such education) expired under the Trump administration. Though that law has been rightfully critiqued for funneling public funds to law enforcement instead of services for survivors of domestic and dating violence, it further puts funding for programs that address intimate partner violence at risk.

Seeing strong, powerful women in the media, on stage, and on screen was exciting for me as a teenager, but even with a burgeoning interest in feminism, I didn't yet have the critical understanding to translate the idea of "empowerment" into actively defining my own life. Without education and places to discuss experiences and to develop a collective, critical consciousness, young people grappling with various forms of oppression may see those who are supposed to represent "empowered role models" as just another unattainable ideal to which they can't quite measure up.

This dynamic became more apparent to me when I attended a special training with my classmates on dating abuse and bullying, presented by four twenty-somethings who identified themselves as our "peers."

"One in three teenagers have been subject to verbal, emotional, physical, or sexual abuse by their dating partners," a woman named Stephanie explained. "Only one third of teens who have

3 cnn.com/2018/09/29/health/sex-education-consent-in-public-schools-trnd/index.html

been in a violent relationship have ever told anyone about it, and most parents believe teen dating violence is not an issue."

According to loveisrespect, in 2019 girls and young women between the ages of 16 and 24 experienced the highest rate of intimate partner violence, which is almost triple the national average,[4] a statistic similar to those which Stephanie shared in her presentation in the 1990s.

"So, what is abuse?" continued Jeffrey, looking at us meaningfully, "We're going to do a few role plays to help illustrate."

"I wish you wouldn't wear your hair like that," Jeffrey quipped. "You look so much better when you wear it down. You look ugly like that."

Their conversation escalated, back and forth, until their play fully consisted of phrases like "I'm going to punch a hole in the wall if you keep hanging out with those friends," and "It's your fault I'm like this, if you didn't act like this I wouldn't get so jealous and angry," then, "I need you. I'll kill myself if you break up with me."

The presentation felt like it was talking directly to me. I was dumbfounded. Hadn't Link told me that he needed my presence in his life to feel better? I had been flattered *then*. He had made me feel important and needed. When I'd mentioned Link's jealousy to friends they'd shrugged it off; "Guys can be sensitive and weird." Link was very emotional and depressed, but I had thought that had made him deep, like the troubled

---

4 loveisrespect.org/resources/dating-violence-statistics/

grunge icons we were supposed to venerate, like Nirvana's Kurt Cobain and Evan Dando, the lead singer of the alternative band the Lemonheads who was in and out of rehab for heroin use, and fictional characters like Jordan Catalano on alterna-teen drama *My So Called Life*, who was ambivalent about and often ignored the main character played by Claire Danes, but would occasionally make out with her in the school's basement. These icons and the men who emulated them embraced a softer model of masculinity, which seemingly made them more sensitive and more in touch with their "feminine" side, but did not actually give up or question the power they had as straight, white men or become critical about how sexism shaped their expectations for women and themselves. As I thought through Stephanie and Jeffrey's play I realized the "sensitivity" in guys my friends had shrugged off had other names: manipulation and abuse.

While Riot Grrrl music had shown me a fierce model of femininity, and training programs like the one I experienced shared some tools for addressing abusive behavior of men towards women, this didn't automatically translate into "empowerment." I, like many of my peers, was caught in a paradox of who girls, especially middle class suburban girls, were supposed to be in the 1990s: strong and sassy, but still nice and not rude; cute and original, but still pretty and not slutty; smart, but still non-threatening. It was this conundrum that formed the thesis of Mary Pipher's bestselling book *Reviving Ophelia: Saving the Selves of Adolescent Girls*. The book spoke to the changes that young women often went through during adolescence: from strong, self-assured, and self-confident to self-effacing, plagued by depression and eating disorders, and "at risk" for underage drinking, drugs, and sex.

A middle-aged, white, well-meaning feminist therapist, Pipher contended that sexism was a cause of young women's struggles, but her individualized case studies focused more on the individual role that parents and authorities could play in the lives of young women. She did not fully address the systemic issues that caused young women to conform to sexist social pressure.

This individualized approach put pressure back on young women to resist sexism alone, as opposed to collectively and reinforced a neo-liberal feminist idea that sexism could be solved through individual "empowerment." Andi Zeisler describes the logic of this shift that occurred in the late 1980s to mid-1990s in her book *We Were Feminists Once*: "The insidiousness of second-generation gender bias—informal exclusion, lack of mentors and role models, fear of conforming to stereotypes—colluded with the ideological spread of neoliberalism to recast institutional inequity as mere personal challenges. If women now had the right to do most everything a man could do, went the logic, then any obstacles or failures weren't systemic, they were individual and could be remedied by simply being better, faster, stronger, wealthier."[5] It also reflected an overall cultural panic over young women's autonomy, sexuality, and identity in the 1990s and posed young women as immature people who needed to be "saved" as opposed to a society that needed to be changed.

"White boy, don't laugh, don't cry, just die!" snarled Kathleen Hanna on Bikini Kill's record *Yeah Yeah Yeah Yeah*.

---

5 Andi Zeisler, *We Were Feminists Once*, New York: Public Affairs, 2016, 155.

For girls like me, Bikini Kill might as well have lived on another planet. Even though they sang about boys making them feel afraid and society making them feel ashamed, their music was fearless, enraged, a force to be reckoned with. They did not give a shit about following the rules or being perfect. No well-meaning middle aged therapist needed to "save" them. In one of her iconic photos, Kathleen Hanna, Bikini Kill's singer, wears a short "schoolgirl" skirt and black bra, SLUT written in block letters across her stomach, and grabs her crotch as she screams into the mic in a small, sweaty punk club. In the 1990s, in our suburban bedrooms, thousands of teenaged girls like me ached to be like her—fierce, cocky, flagrantly feminist, but the way to do so wasn't abundantly clear.

For myself, I wondered how could I be a feminist and a Riot Grrrl if I was afraid to leave Link and scared to be without a boyfriend? Bikini Kill wanted to kill the white boy mentality. Surely, they had no patience for people like me who felt alone and unsure even though they wanted to be brave and badass. Feminism seemed far away, a destination I wanted to reach, but didn't know the way toward.

In addition to albums and bands, through Riot Grrrl I discovered zines—self-published magazines often made by other girls my age that sang the praises of Riot Grrrl bands, gossiped about different band members, and talked deeply about their own lives. They were "messing with what was sacred," in the words of Sleater-Kinney, by disclosing secrets—like boyfriends who had tried to control the type of music they listened to, where they went, who they hung out with, threatening to spread nasty rumors about them or even kill themselves if they didn't comply.

Tensions worsened with Link once I met Asher, a tall, gangly boy with doey brown eyes and floppy brown hair who knew about Sleater-Kinney, loved Sonic Youth, and also played a Fender guitar. Asher invited me over to jam and soon we started an experimental punk band. I shrugged off Asher's comment that I was a part of the band because having a girl playing guitar was "cool," because joining a band meant I could leap across a chasm between the punk feminist I wanted to become and the punk feminist I didn't quite feel capable of yet.

My announcement that I was going to be in a band sent Link into a jealous rage. On a late August afternoon we sat on my bedoorm's beige carpet, talking with strained voices. Piles of my CDs and notebooks containing songs I had started to write were stacked near my stereo, and a pile of zines sat near my bed. I tried to explain to him for the upteenth time that just because I liked music and zines made by women didn't mean I didn't like him.

"Can't you see that it's taking you away from me!" he yelped, lunging at my notebooks, grabbing on and trying to tear them in half. Unsuccessful, he flailed towards the pile of CDs, flinging them at me as I covered my face. Their sharp plastic cases glanced off my forearms before scattering all over the rug. "Stoppit!" I shrieked, as he stormed out with a muffled cry.

When he called me later that night, as he always did at 8:30, he started to plead with me. "If you didn't listen to this music and try to be in bands I wouldn't be so mad. You are making me like this. I can't lose you."

"You introduced me to this. You taught me to play guitar. This is the stuff you like. I don't understand why you don't like it," I shot back, still not quite comprehending how radical feminism could be so threatening to a supposedly "sensitive" guy.

"It wasn't supposed to be for you! Without you I don't know what I'll do with my life. I don't want to lose you. I'll kill myself. Please just stop listening to those CDs and playing electric guitar and I promise I will stop being upset."

Nausea swept over me. I was exhausted. I thought back to the roleplay that Stephanie and Jeffrey had presented at school. I thought about the girls whose zines I had read who had had the courage to leave their abusive boyfriends, and how I could make a zine to add my story to theirs. I thought about the band Asher and I were going to start and how I could finally make music I wrote instead of just listening to others. Finally, the future felt full enough without Link.

I took a deep breath.

I set *Call the Doctor* into the CD tray and the music wailed from the stereo speakers.

> *"A cheap little ring / a cute little house / the deal is cut and dried / not for sale / not your girl / not your thing / you've got me mixed up with somebody else!"*

"Don't call me anymore," I said, hands shaking, and placed the beige plastic phone onto the receiver.

A BRAVE GIRLS' WORLD

"*I will resist with every inch and every breath / I will resist this psychic death!*" Bikini Kill wailed on their early song and Riot Grrrl rallying cry "Resist Psychic Death." Songs like this one illustrated how sexism was as common as the air we breathe and a key part of liberation is coming to consciousness. Feminism, as understood through the lens of Riot Grrrl, was about being who you were without apology, being loud, and taking up space. It was the sound of distorted guitars, rage, and defiance against all that young women were supposed to be and achieve. I was determined to be part of this young shift in the feminist movement that political commentators were calling "the third wave."

While many feminist organizers, particularly women of color, fall outside of the definition of the "waves," in general the "first wave" referred to the movement for women's rights that began at the Seneca Falls Convention on Women's Rights in 1848 and lasted through the suffrage movement. The second wave refers to the feminist movement of the 1960s and 70s, inspired by the Civil Rights and Anti-War movements. Black feminism developed in the 70s and 80s, seemingly "between" the waves. Black feminists, along with other feminists of color, practiced a politics of intersectionality, a phrase that was coined by Kimberlé Crenshaw in 1989. The ideas behind an intersectional approach to feminist politics were articulated over a decade earlier by the radical, Black socialist Combahee River Collective. In their now-iconic 1977 statement they wrote, "... we are actively committed to struggling against racial, sexual, heterosexual, and class oppression, and see as our particular task the development of integrated analysis and practice based upon the fact that the major systems of oppression are interlocking."[6] This intersectional approach to feminism, as well as an anti-essentialist approach, provided much of the underpinnings of third wave feminism.

However, third wave feminism also emphasized a rhetoric of "choice" when it came to how feminist politics were practiced. In her introduction to *To be Real,* an anthology of essays that is often cited as helping define the third wave of feminism, Rebecca Walker explained, "The greatest gift we can give one another is the power to make a choice. The power to choose is even more important than the choices we make."[7] The third wave's emphasis on "choice" as a defining feature of their interpretation of feminism made the movement vulnerable to a neoliberal, capitalist idea that "choice feminism" equals "consumer choice." However, this expansive approach to feminism was meant to reject the perceived essentialist notions of womanhood and gender, the idea that there was a correct way to be a feminist, and embrace a complex feminism with multiple interpretations. Third wave feminism acknowledged that people inhabited and celebrated multiple identities, especially shaped by race, class, gender expression, and sexuality.

In her preface to *To Be Real,* second-wave feminist icon Gloria Steinem tried to explain to readers that feminism had always been more of a multiplicity than the popular imagination allowed, but in the 1990s, "the idea that there is or ever was one 'right' way to

---

6 Keeanga-Yamahtta,Taylor, Ed. *How We Get Free: Black Feminism and the Combahee River Collective,* Chicago, Haymarket Books, 2017, p. 15.
7 Rebecca Walker, ed. *To be real: Telling the truth and changing the face of feminism,* Anchor Books, 1995, p. xxvi.

be a feminist has become more prevalent," which she attributed both to media backlash against feminism and to a growing, diverse feminist movement. "As a result," she explained, "people working on equality now are much more likely to come together around a particular issue, profession, or shared experience, and thus to be vulnerable to the idea that the mythical movement of 'real' feminists is somewhere else."[8] In addition, as Sara Marcus explains in *Girls to the Front,* her history of the Riot Grrrl movement, as mainstream feminism in the early 1990s turned towards middle-of-the-road electoral politics and critiquing the lack of women in seats of corporate power, Riot Grrrl and the third wave appealed to the more immediate concerns of young women. She explained, "When you're a teenage girl who's trying with all your might not to hate yourself, trying not to get harassed or raped, trying not to let bikini blondes in beer ads crush your self-image, trying not to be discouraged from joining a sports team or math club or shop class or school newspaper, trying not to let your family's crippling dysfunction (and the confounding irony of enduring domestic cruelty in an age of Family Values) make you want to fucking *die,* a feminist movement that's mostly about electing new Senators might not be all that compelling to you."[9]

Walker's insistence on the importance of feminist choice also highlighted another important part of the third wave feminist moment: it was couched in the personal and cultural experience as central to an understanding of feminism and coming into politics. This approach was a bold, in-your-face response to hand

---

8 Steinem in Walker, p. Xvii.
9 Sara Marcus, *Girls to the Front,* New York: Harper Perennial, 2010, 26.

wringing from some second wave feminists that there "were no young feminists." This approach was summed up in second wave feminist Phillis Chesler's book *Letters to a Young Feminist*, published in 1997, where she attempts to claim overnership over a younger generation of feminists who are embodying feminism differently than many white, radical second wave women did. The third wave was also pushing back against prevalent media stereotypes of feminists as man-hating, humorless "femi-Nazis," in the language of popular right wing radio commentator Rush Limbaugh, who my Dad liked to listen to and chuckle along to. Punk and Riot Grrrl showed me, and a generation of young women, that we could not only seize the means of cultural production through making our own zines, playing in bands, and finding spaces on the burgeoning internet, but also craft identities for ourselves that challenged stereotypes of who women and feminists could be.

While I felt distant from real-life Riot Grrrls and the Riot Grrrl movement seemed almost mythic to me, I embraced the idea of the "third wave" that feminism could be what you made of it. As a young feminist I felt I had the freedom to do so, even if I lacked an in-person feminist community. Riot Grrrl-style provided a framework through which I decided to organize my life. If feminist writers like Walker could insist we could choose what our feminism looked like and Riot Grrrl bands like Bikini Kill encouraged their listeners to embrace their own power and vulnerability, singing, "Dare ya to do what you want / Dare ya to be who you will / Dare ya to cry right out loud," I was ready to be part of it.

To be a feminist and Riot Grrrl and find others like me, I decided first I needed to look like one, style and looks being the most accessible and the most in my control as a teenager. Riot Grrrl fashion drew from the earlier punks styles of plaid, fishnets, and safety pins, combined with a grungy, thrift store aesthetic. The goal of the style was your own representation and sexuality, often expressed through short skirts and crop tops, and reclaiming "girlish" accessories and aesthetics like barrettes or Hello Kitty, as a way to be soft and tough. To try to achieve this, I had a friend cut the wavy hair that flowed down my back to a chin-length bob, which then poofed out into an unfortunate triangle thanks to my curly hair. I tamed it with bright, plastic hair barrettes designed for little girls, which, as I had seen in pictures, were a Riot Grrrl favorite. In my bathroom, armed with plastic gloves and a jar of Manic Panic hair dye (which offered a range of day-glo-like colors and was widely available in "alternative" record stores and mall shops like Hot Topic), I spread globby, bright pink goo on my hair, tucked it under a shower cap, blasted it with a hair dryer, and waited. For weeks I left neon rose residue on my pillows and shirt collars, but my short curls bounced bright pink and proud.

I was hoping that my fashion would signal to other girls that Riot Grrrls were present in Maine and draw them to me. Despite my isolation, I didn't realize until I read *Girls to the Front* in the mid-2010s that this was actually a common experience of many involved in or aware of Riot Grrrl—even those like Sara Marcus, the book's author, who lived close to the centers of Riot Grrrl activity like Washington DC, felt like the movement was hard to find or happening without them. Marcus describes "missing out" on the first few years of Riot Grrrl and discusses writing "R-I-

O-T G-I-R-L" across her knuckles. "I waited to see another one. I waited to stumble into a whole pack of them. I wanted for a gang to stop me and say, 'You're coming with us.'"[10]

Riot Grrrl wasn't just fashion, though. It was also finding methods to showcase your voice and experience as a girl. Riot Grrrl felt like permission to step up and claim our dreams for ourselves. For me, that meant claiming my identity as a writer, even though I knew no "real" publisher would be interested. As the next step in my Riot Grrrl transformation, I spent the remainder of my summer sitting on my parent's porch, painstakingly typing diary entries about the emotional manipulation and abuse I had experienced in my relationship with Link on my mother's navy blue, electric, Smith-Corona typewriter. I included quotes from Sleater-Kinney and Bikini Kill rendered in letter stamps with a curlicue font and poems I'd written for English class, and collaged them onto pages ripped from French Vogue and Delia's clothing catalogues. I asked my Dad if I could use the photocopier in his office and on a quiet August Saturday, after hours of learning how to clear paper jams, my hands streaked with black toner, I held the first forty copies of *Indulgence*, my personal zine, in my hands. Along with my new band, I decided, this would launch me into an artistic, feminist world.

With the launch of my zine, the mailbox became my lifeline. I wrote maniacally to the young women who poured their lives out onto the pages of their zines with titles like *Hope, My New Gun, Housewife Turned Assassin, ¡Mamasita!, Pink Tea, You Might As Well Live,* and *Go Teen Go*. I waited on their letters like glitter and

10 Marcus, 7.

Hello Kitty-sticker covered missives from a distant world. Every day I ran out to the aluminum letterbox on the quiet stretch of country road in front of my family's yellow farmhouse, hoping for news from the world beyond the rolling green hay fields and wooded mountains.

Personal zine culture rose with Riot Grrrl and the advent of the internet in the mid-to-late 1990s. At the time, there were few media outlets, both in print and online, that showcased the unfiltered voices of women and girls. Zines filled a gap and enabled women who didn't see themselves represented in mainstream media (which was quickly consolidating through a series of major media outlet mergers) to control the means of media production, construct their own image, and tell their own stories. As Celia Perez wrote in her zine *I Dreamed I was Assertive,* "I am a zinester of color. I'm Mexican-Cuban-American and I make a zine... I like to think that in putting out a zine I am part of this community of people who have taken publishing into our own hands because we feel that our view and interest are neglected by the mainstream media, because we have a voice that is not being heard."[11] Zines enabled a chorus of brave voices to rise from photocopied pages, and the personal zine subculture that arose out of and was influenced by Riot Grrrl was mostly created by and for women.

While zine makers and Riot Grrrl-inspired feminists connected and chatted on the internet, and some later launched online diaries and blogs, the zines they made and the relationships they formed were the focus. Internet destinations like the message

11 Celia Perez, *I Dreamed I Was Assertive*, Chicago, Self-published, 2000.

boards run by Olympia-based queer feminist Chainsaw records and Pander Zine Distro, run by a zinemaker named Ericka, enabled young women who made zines to form communities and share information more quickly and publically than through the mail alone.

The tone of the zines was often confessional and the audience was mostly other women. It was an opportunity to deconstruct and rage against the perfection we were supposed to pursue as girls and the ideals of sexist, racist, and heterosexist mainstream culture. In addition, zines enabled young women to express themselves and connect with each other through a format that was detached from the toxic trolling culture that would later take over some social media platforms.

While personal zines served as a precursor to confessional social media culture that saturates our lives now via blogs and social media platforms, zines were stubbornly uncommercial. They were part of a long history of self-publishing which some historians connect to Martin Luther's 1517 "95 Theses," which led to the Protestant Reformation and were spread thanks to the then-recent invention of the printing press, and Thomas Paine's pamphlet *Common Sense*, which advocated American independence from the British in 1776. Zines in the 1990s also had their roots in science fiction "fanzines" published in the 1930s, political and underground newspapers and chapbooks from 1950s and 60s counter cultural movements, and punk music zines from the 70s and 80s. With the rise of the photocopier, self-publishing became even more accessible and many zines were more personal, confessional, and free form than traditional magazines. For the most part, zines were a labor of love by their creators. Some companies experimented with making zines to try to achieve a kind of grungy-cool, and some zines accepted advertising to cover production costs, but mostly zines were a platform for the passions and experiences of the people creating them. While mainstream culture did take an interest in zines, with magazines like *Sassy* including a "Zine of the Month" column and coverage in newspapers like the *Washington Post*, unlike blogs in the 2000s or social media influencer culture, they were rarely a ladder to fame, fortune, or cultural influence beyond a very limited subculture. Instead, this coverage by mainstream media often encouraged more young people to launch their own zine.

Reading zines reminded me there was a world of brave girls in the world beyond Portland, Maine. I craved a girl utopia, where it was safe to be myself and who I wanted to become. I never wanted what happened to me with Link to happen again to me or any other girl, and I wanted the same expansive space for the girls whose letters arrived daily in my mailbox. My pen-pals wrote about the injustices large and small they faced at school, at home, at work, and on the street with glittering pink gel pen and bubbly handwriting, and embraced girliness and strength as they wrote their way into feminism. However, in the late 1990s—similar to Sara Marcus and other Riot Grrrls—I felt like there had been a giant grrrl party that I had missed. I read about girls who lived in cities like Berkley and Ithaca who were part of radical queer youth groups, ran record labels, and played in bands. I dreamed of girl bands, girl pirates, girl gangs, anarchist girl collectives, communities of girl artists.

In zines I had read about Riot Grrrl chapters, which were groups of young women who got together to discuss issues in their lives and plan actions to address them. They volunteered to escort women getting abortions at clinics targeted by pro-life protests, organized and attended Take Back the Night rallies and marches against rape and dating violence, and put together girl conventions and gatherings as a way to bring together young feminists. While older generations of feminists wrung their hands and proclaimed, "there are no younger feminists!" the women I read about in zines were creating and practicing a feminism that reflected their current view of world and looked forward instead of back to the second wave of feminist movement. They were, in Rebecca Walker's words, creating spaces where they could be real.[12] While I also absorbed an idealistic vision of these spaces, zines also documented the way they were rarely consistent or coherent and often fractured along race and class lines. I knew feminism was more than what you wore or what music you listened to, but there was no Riot Grrrl group I could join near me. The closest equivalent I could find was the peer-to-peer training group that had given me my first wake up call about my boyfriend's controlling behaviour.

While the group seemed very mainstream to my aspiring punk rock feminism, the idea of raising awareness of domestic and dating violence outside of specific feminist circles was relatively new. Domestic abuse did not become a federal crime until 1994 when Bill Clinton signed the Violence Against Women Act into law and a slew of reports, changes in how law enforcement

---

12 Walker, xI

was supposed to handle domestic violence, and funding for domestic violence prevention followed. However, Clinton's "Crime Bill," unfortunately also expanded the death penalty and the construction of new prisons, ended inmate education, and increased police surveillance of low-income communities of color. This should have resulted in feminist protest against the bill, but I heard little about it until much later, when I learned more about intersectional feminism in college.[13] Groups like the ones I was a part of worked to remove the stigma around being a survivor, believe and validate those who had experienced partner violence, and demand that law enforcement, schools, and social service agencies provide more resources and handle partner violence cases with greater sensitivity and seriousness.

During the group's training sessions I sat nervously in a circle of local teenagers to talk about how power, privilege, manipulation, and bullying worked. Learning about the slow, deliberate work of educating others about the intersections of power and privilege in their own lives isn't the same as the spark of recognition and burning immediacy listening to bands like Sleater-Kinney and Bikini Kill invoked. When your favorite bands are singing about revolution, but you learn about and feel first hand the massive, interconnected structures of power that keep injustice in place, it can be incredibly difficult to understand what can really make a difference and how to live out your ideals, and reality often feels like it falls short. Riot Grrrl felt so immediately accessible to many young women because it helped connect personal actions

---

13 Keeanga-Yamahtta Taylor, *From #BLACKLIVESMATTER to Black Liberation*, Chicago, Haymarket Books, 2016.

with a wider idea and feeling of changing society and not waiting for permission or recognition from an older generation.

Trying to work within the structure of education and nonprofits to create sustainable change felt slow and disconnected from Riot Grrrl's urgency. These types of tensions are inherent to social movements and also to our lives as political beings because our consciousness and political identities evolve, as do wider social and political circumstances. Of course, it's not about finding the "perfect" way to be an activist, but finding what makes the most sense for you and understanding that will evolve over time.

The power of music and art is that it can facilitate those moments of community and connection. I was about to turn 18 when I found out Sleater-Kinney were playing in Boston, about two hours away from my hometown. When they took the stage, I was standing a mere three feet from these women who seemed like untouchable heroes. They had translated my feelings into lyrics and jagged guitar riffs. I was surrounded by girls pushing, jumping up and down, and singing along at full volume. I felt all my sadness, anger, isolation, and insecurity melt as Sleater-Kinney thundered through their songs. The basement club could barely contain the energy as our screams and tears converged together, a relief from the world's relentless sexism, a temporary passport to girl utopia.

Like many young people who find an identity and community that resonates with who they feel they are and aspire to be, my enthusiasm for feminism made me feel incredibly idealistic about its potential in my life. I decided my break with a sexist experience would be definitive. Once I had decided to fully identify with and embody feminism, I was convinced my life would be automatically radically altered. In embracing the aesthetics and practices of third-wave, punk feminism I also treated it as a static destination I could reach. This kind of bold, youthful, far-reaching feminism felt so right and resonated with me so deeply I had a hard time seeing that others around me might not share my enthusiasm. While I embraced the complexity of third wave thinking, I also had an overly simplistic view of the power of simply declaring myself a feminist in my life. The reality, of course, turned out to be more fraught and complicated than I imagined.

REVOLUTION GIRL STYLE NOW

In the early 1990s, Riot Grrrl seemed like an energetic movement riding the surge of punk and grunge culture into the mainstream, guitars loaded with treble and fuzz pedals blazing. By the spring of 1999, however, Riot Grrrl felt like a cultural footnote, no matter what *Spin* magazine had written, and more a musical subgenre than an international, young feminist movement. Summarizing this feeling, Sara Marcus wrote in the epilogue of *Girls To The Front* that by the mid-1990s there was a general feeling Riot Grrrl was passé because, "The media attention had killed it, people said. Or grunge had killed it, or Courtney Love had killed it, or maybe it had never existed in the first place except as a mirage dreamed up by the press."[14] Of course, as Marcus' book illustrates, this was far from the truth and Riot Grrrl, and young feminist energy, could be found in pockets all over the United States. However, in mainstream music and pop culture the Spice Girls, and then Britney Spears, were flaunting a manufactured, pop-perfect, and often very white version of femininity.

The idea of "girl power" had been co-opted to be more about girl's power to be attractive to men and less about demanding equality and equity. The power of diversity and "choice" that third wave feminism offered had been distorted into a neo-liberal idea about the power to choose as consumers in a marketplace. Feminism was no longer about questioning and choosing different tactics to change power structures, but being "empowered" to make a "choice." As Andi Zeisler notes, "Empowerment was also, notably,

---

14 Sara Marcus, *Girls to the Front*, New York, Harper Perennial, 2010, 325.

a softer way to talk about actual power—something that girls in particular are traditionally socialized away from."[15] She explains that within this emerging marketplace, pop-culture feminist lite, embodied by acts like the Spice Girls and sanitized calls for "girl power," "the significant difference was that where Riot Grrrl's vision of empowerment was inherently self-sufficient—Why *not* start a band or make a zine with your friends?—girl power was centered on empowerment by way of the market. What girl power meant in a post-Riot Grrrl world was simply whatever elevated girls as consumers."[16]

The co-option and commodification of third wave feminism by mainstream culture is one way a sexist culture moved to dismiss that which threatened it. However, I still wanted a girl utopia close to home. The Riot Grrrl chapters I had read about sounded like 1970s consciousness-raising circles crossed with punk's raucous, anti-authoritarian spirit, and I wanted to feel that in my life on a more regular basis. Entering my senior year of high school, I decided to take the DIY spirit I'd learned from punk to heart and start my own feminist, activist organization. Lilias, a dedicated Hole fan that had come with me to Boston to see Sleater-Kinney, agreed to start it with me. Together we wanted to build a tangible, young feminist presence in our hometown.

The idea that Riot Grrrl seemed like a passé subculture to others filled me with motivation — I'll show them, I thought. Having an ally close to home suddenly made all the difference. I was determined to engage in my own version of feminism, not just

15 Zeisler, 172.
16 Zeisler, 177.

pine for it. Lilias and I spent the next few weeks handing out flyers to other girls at punk shows and leaving them in bookstores and cafes. We had no idea who would show up, but we hoped our call for young feminist activists would resonate with other young women and they'd be brave enough to come forward to join us.

Organizing, like making art, feels uncertain, like trying to conjure the concrete from the elusive, like a shared sentiment, experience, or cultural phenomenon. One of the most powerful tenants of DIY feminism that I absorbed from Riot Grrrl was not to wait for permission to create change—to take a risk to stand up for what I believed in. Despite having participated in the anti-domestic violence group and my high school's Gay/Straight Alliance, like any young, aspiring organizer, I still had a lot to learn. On the day of our first meeting I realized in panic that I had neglected to make a concrete agenda for the meeting. After introductions I looked at Lilias awkwardly as silence filled the gallery and asked, "What should we discuss today?" I had thought our passion, or at least interest, in feminism would be enough to unite us, but I was starting to realize I knew very little about how to run a cohesive, impactful group.

"What about volunteering to help get out the vote against the proposed anti-abortion legislation that's on the upcoming November ballot?" Lilias suggested. This was legislation that was being considered in Maine to ban the medically incorrect term "partial birth abortion" that had been pushed onto the ballot thanks to organizing by conservative Christian groups. The legislation was part of a broader cultural backlash against expanding civil rights for LGBTQ people and abortion access for women that was working its way through local and state governments all over the country.

There were slow mumbles of consent from the group, but no one came forward with suggestions for concrete action. Lilias passed around a sheet to sign up for phone banking to get out the word about the vote, but when it came back to us I noticed only about half the girls had signed up. I was confused by the lack of engagement in the group and wasn't sure of my role or our overall goals other than to be feminists together. This was not the punk attitude, the storming of the barricades of the political establishment I was hoping for. I also didn't realize I couldn't just assume solidarity because we were girls and that we might need to develop greater trust before jumping into organizing together.

However, this disconnect between identifying as a feminist and taking action was not limited to our group. Mimi Nguyen writes about how in the mid 1990s at a Riot Grrrl show in Berkley, California she asked for volunteers from the over 200 audience members to escort women at an abortion clinic and was resolutely ignored. She wrote, "After you screamed your songs and strutted your bad-ass punk attitudes and paraded your slogans like so much cheap costume jewelry, I was left standing talking as if underwater or in Vietnamese."[17] This lack of concrete or consistent political engagement raised a question about Riot Grrrl-inspired feminism: was the purpose simply to bring young feminist women together to talk about their lives and feel less alone (though as Mimi pointed out, this was often

---

17 Mimi Nguyen, *Slant 5*, in Darms, 307.

limited to majority-white, middle class women), or was it to take politically-inspired action based on solidarity?

"Any other issues that you have been thinking about that you would like to discuss?" I asked.

"I think," said Anna, who had been involved in environmental activism since she was a child, and exuded an air of political savvy that I secretly envied, "That we all wish we were in Seattle right now."

The news had been full of reports from the streets of Seattle, which were clogged with giant puppets, Teamsters, anarchists, environmentalists dressed like sea turtles, and phalanxes of flannel-shirted activists all protesting the World Trade Organization meetings. There were also armies of officers that looked like stormtroopers in full black riot gear facing up against them. Tanks rumbled down the usually placid downtown streets while tear gas billowed like fog. The diversity of the activists and causes that had come together to advocate for global economic justice looked much more like the ideal of full-on social "revolution" than the punk-inflected "revolution grrrl style now" that obsessed me.

Thanks to the protests, I had just learned a new word, and a new cause: "anti-globalization." But while I might have raged against sweatshop labor practices where women and children worked long hours in hot, dangerous factories sewing Nikes and other Western luxury goods, I was too embarrassed to admit as Anna spoke that I didn't quite understand yet how global trade could be a feminist issue, as I had been so focused on issues that impacted the day-to-day personal lives of young women like myself. However, current statistics estimate that 90% of employees of sweatshops are women ages 15 to 22 who are paid as little as six cents an hour.[18] Women in unsafe labor conditions are also vulnerable to sexual harassment, abuse, and are often fired for being pregnant. As I learned more about the inequities in global trade and the colonial histories that shaped them, I sheepishly realized that the girl utopia and revolution that I had dreamed of seemed completely based on the world I knew in the United States. While Riot Grrrl reached girls around the world — for example, I had penpals from Belgium, Italy, the UK, Mexico, Australia, and the Philippines — and punk as a subculture more broadly has had a profound impact on youth culture across the globe, the personal-experience-focused philosophy of Riot Grrrl did not immediately translate into understanding the complexity of global politics and power. Girl-style revolution was a lot harder than we thought and punk feminism had not given us a framework to fully understand how to fully enact intersectional-minded struggles against oppression. Change didn't just happen because you wanted it to. Or as Mimi Nguyen wrote in 1994, "Girl power t-shirts a revolution it doesn't make, honey and I learned it doesn't make for a revolutionary, either."[19] Actual revolution girl style was slow work, and I wasn't sure I had the patience. However, to face a global reality, my feminist practice had to evolve.

18 Feminist Majority Foundation, "Feminists Against Sweatshops," accessed February 9, 2020. feminist.org/other/sweatshops/index.html
19 Nguyen in Darms, 307.

Phone banking to get out the vote against the anti-abortion proposal felt far less glamorous than the ideal of punk grrrl revolution I'd carried around with me. I knew intellectually that social change came from a series of small actions, but before then had not fully accepted the reality of what those small gestures would look and feel like. On a Tuesday night I sat in the basement of a local non-profit with Anna and Lilias by my side, my jaw clenched with fear everytime I dialed a new phone number. When someone answered I tried not to fumble over my script and reminded myself this was all for the cause of being a feminist. As I reminded Democrats to get out the vote, I learned that some even supposed-progressives were hostile to women's rights and reproductive freedom. I felt a sense of relief when the anti-abortion legislation failed to pass, but keeping Maine's reproductive freedom law the same hardly felt like a victory. Riot Grrrl, and punk in general, mostly tended to ignore, if not carry outright disdain for, the traditional US political establishment and the party system. As a movement, Riot Grrrl was focused on the lives, experiences, and creativity of young women, and while those were clearly impacted by policy, politicians, and legislation, grrrls most often did not make democratic political change their main focus. As a result, while Riot Grrrl had an impact on culture, music, aesthetics, and fashion, it did not translate into traditional political power and, in many ways, that was never the aim.

The long term vision activism and organizing requires was rarely discussed during Riot Grrrl, but engagement with local issues can have a tangible and more immediate impact, even if it doesn't feel like idealized "revolution." After the 2016 election in the United States there was a surge of political volunteering, canvassing, and phone banking, much of it by women, for progressive candidates and issues, as well as a surge of women running for, and winning, offices across the country. With a Republican controlled Senate, there was also an increased focus on local issues and protecting rights for women, immigrants, and LGBTQ people at the local level. Local legislation can have a huge impact on the way people live their lives daily, as well as help set a precedent for federal legislation. While the individual work it takes to support local candidates and legislation (as well as build a base around progressive politics) can feel small, the upsurge in political activity since 2016 is also a reminder that collectively, over time, these actions can significantly contribute to social change. They can also contribute to social uprising and mass movement, which can bring about swifter change in culture, legislation, and consciousness, as demonstrated by the Black Lives Matter protests that blossomed across the world in the summer of 2020.

While Riot Grrrl had helped me think very personally about feminism, as a new activist, I had been naive about the mechanics of legislative politics and community organizing. Without mentorship, radical role models, or the understanding that organizing was a lifelong process that would develop over time, our feminist group quickly fizzled out. While there had been increased attention throughout the 1990s about the need for girls to develop "leadership skills" and encourage their participation in politics, there was not widespread education for girls and young women about how to meaningfully engage in them. Similar to the emphasis on "empowerment" Andi Zeisler commented on as a softer way to talk about power, training girls for "leadership" was also a way to ignore critique of the capitalist, sexist, racist structures of power that defined "leadership qualities" as associated with rich, white men, and prevented women and girls from thriving in the first place. The women leaders we may have noticed on a national level, like Madeline Albright or even then-First Lady Hillary Clinton, were piloried in the media and popular culture as sexless, brassy, bossy bitches who had run afoul in a world of men. Hardly encouraging for young women who might aspire to political office or challenge what "leadership" looked like one day.

One reason the Riot Grrrl model of feminism seemed so compelling to young feminists was its sense of emotional urgency, compelling relatability, and the emotional immediacy of the effect it cultivated. It was centered on personal expression and transformation in girls' daily lives and so that was the experience of feminism I had focused on at first. And while Riot Grrrl and third wave feminism seemed to set themselves apart from earlier practices and expressions of feminism, for many young women in the 1990s, unless our mothers had been involved in the movement or we took women studies classes in college, there was very little information readily available about what different aspects of that movement had looked like. Backlash against feminism throughout the 1980s had been swift and severe, so even young feminists tended to inherit stereotypes of the older feminism generation as being humorless, man hating, and culturally homogenous. While I had bought a copy of *Our Bodies, Ourselves*, published by the feminist Boston Women's Health Collective, I didn't know about their organizing or origins, or other feminist collective projects, like Kitchen Table Women of Color Press, even though I would have benefitted immensely from their work. Overall, the politics espoused by many Riot Grrrls could be alienating to women of color and many zines written by women of color, such as *Slant* and *Slander* by Mimi Nguyen, *Quantify* and *You Might As Well Live* by Lauren Martin, and *¡Mamasita!* by Bianca Ortiz, among many others, critiqued Riot Grrrl's approach to race and racism. These writers called white women out for centering their own experiences in meetings, appropriating cultural practices and styles from communities of color, and being blind to their own privilege. To really understand how to create social change it was important to reach beyond the confines of punk rock or a specific subculture.

Many young women often referred to the writing of bell hooks' *Talking Back: Thinking Feminist, Thinking Black*. She had been referenced in zines as required reading, especially for white feminists who were trying to "work on their shit" around race and racism. Fueled with intellectual firepower, her words on the intersection of race, gender and sexuality, and how feminism as practiced by many white women excluded women of color, tore into my consciousness. She outlined how, while the central feminist idea of "having a voice" was important, black women often were anything but silent, but because of the intersection of sexism and racism they were rarely listened to.

hooks was also critical of the way feminism had been taken up by mainstream culture to become focused on specific women's individual voices or achievements. She wrote,

> "To speak as an act of resistance is quite different than ordinary talk, or the personal confession that has no relation to coming into political awareness, to developing

critical consciousness. This is a difference we must talk about in the United States, for here the idea of finding a voice risks being trivialized or romanticized in the rhetoric of those who advocate a shallow feminist politic which privileges acts of speaking over the content of speech."[20]

hooks made a subtle point about how feminism did not automatically equal women asserting themselves or "having a voice." It meant understanding how power operated unequally and working for collective liberation, not individual success. While hooks was fiercely critical, she wasn't bitter. She outlined an alternate future where justice and equality could be a reality and had the audacity to acknowledge that it might be possible to get there. Most critically, hooks helped push a wide understanding of intersectional feminism with her description of mainstream, US culture and systems of power as a white supremacist, capitalist patriarchy. Defining the structures in which we live also gives us ammunition to dismantle them.

Further pushing forward an understanding of the intersections between intersectional feminism and an anti-capitalist struggle was trans author Leslie Feinberg, who was often quoted in zines and referenced in Team Dresch lyrics as a queer icon. Using gender-neutral pronouns, ze described hirself as a "tangled knot of gender." In hir 1998 book *Trans Liberation*, ze wrote about how resisting the gender binary and the straightjacket that gendered expectations put us in would liberate and benefit all, not just those who identified as trans, writing "Trans liberation has

---

20 hooks, bell, Talking Back: Thinking Feminist, Thinking Black, Boston: South End Press, 1989, 14.

meaning for you—no matter how you define or express your sex or your gender."[21] Ze wrote about the growing trans liberation movement and connected it to the legacy of consciousness raising and concrete activism of feminists of the 70s, and accurately foresaw how trans activism had the potential to transform society and open up how we think about and live our gender.

In 1999 I saw Leslie Feinberg speak in Lewiston, a fading small city in Maine's own rust belt, reminiscent of the working class towns where ze grew up. I watched hir speak, bald head, square jaw, and broad shoulders, about growing up working class and genderqueer, how hir family had worked in mills much like this one, and the injustice meted out to transgender people. Feinberg asserted that the rights of transgender people, and all people to gender expression, was an important part of the struggle for human rights, and discussed how important it was to build coalitions, not just within the feminist and LGBTQ communites, but between all radical and progressive groups, to work for real political power. Ze asked important questions such as, "How can we weed out all the forms of trans-phobic and gender-phobic discrimination? Where does the struggle for sex and gender liberation fit in relation to other movements for economic and social equality?"[22] Feinberg demonstrated how feminism, when approached from an intersectional perspective and combined with concrete activism and organizing, could be a force to liberate all, no matter what their gender.

---

21 Leslie Feinberg, *Trans Liberation*, Boston: Beacon Press, 1998, 5.
22 Ibid, 12.

While younger activists, like myself as a teenager, may have a lot to learn about the mechanics of organizing, they can also be a source of fresh perspective and energy. Younger activists are leading contemporary movements against police brutality and racist policing practices, climate change, sexual assault, and school violence, often with an intersectional perspective. While some make it to the news, what's significant is the work being done school by school, and town by town. Activism, and community building, is much about experimentation and knowing you don't have to be an expert to try something. Inspired, but also disillusioned by Riot Grrrl and wanting to embrace a fuller vision of social justice motivated by hooks and Feinberg, my final semester of high school I organized a conference to bring together all the different factions of activists in Southern Maine. It started to seem so obvious: capitalism, patriarchy, heterosexism, transphobia, police violence, and the legacy of slavery would never be overthrown if we couldn't listen to each other. I had been inspired by Riot Grrrl and zine related conventions and gatherings, which had been organized in places as varying as Washington DC, San Francisco, Olympia, Omaha, and Bowling Green, Ohio. I had read in zines about how tensions related to race and class often erupted at those conferences and I wanted to learn how to address those issues productively. Punks often sang about "unity" and Riot Grrrls had written about "grrrl love," but did not offer much guidance on what it would take to achieve some kind of unity between activists. They also did not often discuss how the burden of maintaining "unity" often fell on those with less privilege by staying silent about how oppression and power played out in these underground, supposedly liberatory spaces.

I spent that winter contacting speakers, making an agenda, agonizing about how I could use this one day to make a splash in the political community and put myself on the map as an "activist." Like many activists, I was not only driven by a vision for social justice, but also partially by my ego. I hoped the conference would launch me into being a radical activist and cutting edge feminist.

The conference took place at my high school on a sunny Saturday in May. The participants were mostly other high school students that I'd met at punk shows, members of the defunct feminist group, a couple of acquaintances from the anti-dating violence group, and a few classmates who had decided to show up. A women's self-defense instructor led a workshop in a courtyard. We listened to a presentation on the history of black communities in Maine and how to address systemic racism. Food Not Bombs, a collection of anarchist punks who cooked free vegan meals from donated food, served lunch. My grandmother, a devout Irish Catholic who had studied with the Jesuits, checked in conference participants. She didn't bat an eyelash about the seemingly radical agenda that included workshops on transphobia and being an ally to transgender people and on safe sex and radical consent. The evening included a punk show at a Unitarian Universalist church, where we politely listened to two local "political punk" bands we'd all seen at every other benefit show. And that was it.

I was proud of the conference, but also disappointed there wasn't a more tangible result. The immediacy of punk, along with being newly awakened to feminism, didn't lend itself to stepping back and looking at the bigger picture. Bringing people together, and helping to create spaces to exchange information is like planting seeds where you don't always know where or how they'll grow. It's a long game and one that can be at odds with punk's urgency.

Despite that feeling, discovering feminism and Riot Grrrl had given me, and many other young women, a framework for surviving, growing, and starting to come into my own as I began to navigate the world as an adult. It went beyond a bland concept of individualized "self-esteem," which researchers, teachers, and counselors insisted girls needed to develop, and helped me begin to cultivate a critical understanding of how sexism worked to undermine girls, women, men, and gender non-conforming people as well. Identities are especially volatile during our teenage years. At times the feminism of Riot Grrrls and other young people looks like a hodgepodge of contradictory ideas, but that is also due to the fact that our sense of ourselves was still in flux and formation. Our identities are never fixed, a lesson I learned early from my zine pen pals who were experimenting with finding their own and then reinforced by theorists like Judith Butler and the work of writers like Kate Bornstein. As a teenager, punk-inflected feminism gave me the ability to fight for space and advocate for myself and others who were marginalized by the forces of sexism, racism, homophobia, and classism, a skill set which is not automatically offered to young women.

The feminism I found at the end of the 1990s was expansive, intersectional, community-oriented, and motivated by a do-it-yourself spirit. The punk movement had shown me that I could start where I was and not wait for someone else to pronounce me a writer, musician, artist, or activist. It had given me and others like me a tool kit, and high ideals, with which to move through the world and understand how power operated both in intimate relationships and on a global scale, as well as a drive to address those alongside other feminists. It also raised questions that are central to any feminist organizing and community building in any era: how to navigate across difference and find solidarity and common ground to work against oppression; where power is centered and who it centers; the challenge of meeting and engaging people where they are; and how to effectively challenge and critique structures of power and the culture they propped up.

I recognized feminism wasn't perfect, but discovering it had been transformative. At the end of my teens, and the end of my time living in Maine, I still believed girl utopia was possible, and I was ready to venture beyond the confines of my hometown to find a community where it could be.

GIRL UTOPIA FOUND AND LOST

To teenaged punk feminists like me in the year 2000, Portland, Oregon was a beacon of radical possibility. The city was the center of my visions of girl utopia, a place where I imagined girls' and womens' experiences could be centered and I could build a life and identity free of the influence of sexism, racism, and homophobia. I wanted to step off the plane and find my feminist identity fully formed, to be transformed by my new association with the place. Just down the Interstate from Olympia, Washington, one of Riot Grrrl's founding cities, Portland was homebase to feminist bands I idolized, like Sleater-Kinney and Team Dresch. Musicians, activists, and artists had flocked there due to the "do it yourself" creative culture and cheap rent. The city had a history of basement shows, independent record labels, and zine publishing and had hosted a Riot Grrrl convention in 1996 that brought together girls from all over the Pacific Northwest and country for workshops, discussions, and performances that had become the stuff of legend in the zines I read in the late 1990s.

Even though Riot Grrrl itself had faded in Portland, and the city was rapidly becoming more expensive as people moved there in increasing numbers, I wanted to immerse myself in its legacy. I arrived from rural Maine, a newly minted high school graduate, unaware that in addition to the thriving punk scene, strong coffee, and indie book and record stores, the city also boasted a faltering economy and a history of white supremacy and sexual violence often masked as the "pioneer spirit." I had one year to live there before starting college in New York and was intensely focused on finding the version of the city I had imagined. I was determined to meet other queer feminists and jump head first into the community of girl punks, feminist zine publishers, and bike riding activists. I was looking to girls in Portland to show me real life examples of how to fuse my feminist identity with feminist activism and become my guide to a more radical life.

In many ways Portland did resemble the girl utopia I'd dreamed about. One fall night after a bike ride I sat on the Skidmore bluffs with a group of girls, thrift store jackets adorned with silk screened patches, looking over a vast industrial park next to the Willamette river and felt like the city belonged to us. It felt both cozy and challenging, a mix that lulled many of us, despite our interest in radical activism, into thinking that the prevailing values in Portland would easily extend to the rest of the country. While Portland was a politically progressive pocket surrounded by a more conservative state, I was relieved to be in a place where it seemed my very existence as a young woman was not questioned. I felt like being there would give me the opportunity to become who I wanted to be in a community of others who shared my values and politics. However, much like Riot Grrrl had been, the majority, but not entirety, of girls and women involved in the underground scene there were white, and while many of us were inspired by the politics of activists of color, our social circles were fairly racially homogenous. Still, I wanted to figure out who I was as a feminist and what embracing the identity of a "feminist activist" really looked like. I hoped Portland was a place where I could ground myself in feminist community and create my own feminist world. I felt rigidly determined to devise an answer of how to live as a grown-up, radical feminist.

I met Deirdre through trading zines and a punk publishing conference she helped organize. She was loved, feared, and, above all, *known* in the punk feminist zine community. She commanded attention with her wild, fire-engine red hair, mismatched thrift store style that included plaid skirts, fluorescent pink tights, and worn out Doc Martens. Her zine was a densely packed, thickly folded wad of pages, the text banged out on a typewriter, the lines blurring together and as hard to read as they were urgent. She wrote about growing up poor and working class in the Midwest, how she was inspired by the Black Panthers and the Radical Weathermen, and how much she hated dumb white boys. I was drawn in by her sharp writing and her wry, quick snark. She specialized in "calling people out on their shit" and her rants lit up internet message boards devoted to zines and punk. She was ruthless. I was scared out of my wits and in awe of her.

To me, she embodied the kind of charismatic, offer-no-apology and take-no-shit kind of punk feminist activist I desperately wanted to be. When she invited me to help her start a radical feminist art collective inspired by movements and groups like the Guerilla Girls and ACT UP, I was elated. Deirdre and her idea for a group that was part post-Riot Grrrl consciousness raising group, punk girl gang, artist collective, and activist affinity group seemed like a one-way ticket to the girl utopia I dreamed about. It seemed like a way to revive the scrappy, DIY, feminist spirit of Riot Grrrl, drop some of its more problematic baggage, and adapt it for the early 2000s.

At the feminist collective's first meeting, I sat at a scuffed table in the cavernous cafe of Powell's bookstore with a group of young women Deirdre and I had recruited via our zines and handmade fliers posted at bookstores and cafes. They were high school and college students and dropouts, musicians, writers, zine makers, and artists, shy and hopeful, mostly white, but also Asian, Latina, and Black. Many had just arrived in the city from different corners of the country as disparate as Ohio, California, North Dakota, and Hawaii. Collectively, we were looking to forge a sense of feminist community and figure out who we were as artists and people. As we went around the table and introduced ourselves Deirdre looked each person up and down, as if sizing them up for the revolution to come.

Our first action was to write a manifesto to act as a mission statement to guide our newly minted collective. The Riot Grrrl manifesto, originally published in Bikini Kill's zine in the early 1990s, had helped launch the Riot Grrrl movement and captured the kind of political, creative immediacy we were after. The Riot Grrrl manifesto proclaimed,

> "BECAUSE viewing our work as being connected to our girlfriends-politics-real lives is essential if we are gonna figure out how we are doing impacts, reflects, perpetuates, or DISRUPTS the status quo.
>
> BECAUSE we recognize fantasies of Instant Macho Gun Revolution as impractical lies meant to keep us simply dreaming instead of becoming our dreams AND THUS seek to create revolution in our own lives every single day

by envisioning and creating alternatives to the bullshit christian capitalist way of doing things."[23]

Riot Grrrl, and other feminist groups, had started simply by women getting together to share their experiences and create a collective vision of freedom. I wanted to believe our group was also capable of starting a movement. While Riot Grrrl as a movement had been over for several years by then, we were not interested in resurrecting Riot Grrrl, but focused on bringing together radical, feminist vision shaped by punk with art and direct action. Our manifesto was less confrontational than the Riot Grrrl manifesto, but included statements like:

- We believe all art is political

- We turn trash into art

- Art is living, it cannot be contained in galleries or museums

- Art is radical action

- We believe working collectively is a form of catharsis

We dreamed of creating art that was unpretentious, accessible, and politically minded. We knew intellectually that deep structures of power enabled privileged groups greater cultural access to making art that was deemed worthy and important. However, at that moment just claiming art as something we could all access felt filled with enough radical possibility that we felt it was possible to shake these structures at their foundations.

23 "When She Speaks I Hear the Revolution," February 24, 2010, rebelgrrrl.wordpress.com/2010/02/24/the-riot-grrrl-manifesto/.

Moving from our manifesto to brainstorming for our first collective action was a challenge. Deirdre was interested in the direct action tactics of the eco-minded anarchists who had gravitated to Eugene, Oregon, a college town about two hours south of Portland. These activists, who often operated anonymously under the banner of the Earth Liberation Front, or ELF for short, opposed environmental degradation, rapid development, and dependence on fossil fuels. The members of the ELF were overwhelmingly white and male and put forth a very macho idea of what radical, direct action could be. They burned construction equipment, firebombed offices they accused of doing research on genetically modified organisms, and organized encampments known as "tree sits" in old growth forests targeted for logging. Many of these public and dangerous tactics were enabled by members' race, class, and gender privilege. They also attracted FBI surveillance and the label of "domestic terrorists."

In June of 2000 Jeff "Free" Luers set fire to Joe Romania's SUV dealership in Eugene to call attention to climate change and American dependence on fossil fuels. The fire destroyed a new pickup truck and damaged two others. We read about him in the papers because in November of 2000 he was sentenced to a draconian 22 years in prison, which was later reduced to ten.[24] Through their shadowing of the ELF the FBI were able to begin to generate a culture of fear of "terrorists,"[25] and they had already began working with Portland Police as part of a "Joint Terrorism Task Force." Before this, the Portland Police had a long history

---

24 registerguard.com/article/20140406/NEWS/304069982
25 Alleen Brown, "The Green Scare," The Intercept, March 23, 2019, theintercept.com/2019/03/23/ecoterrorism-fbi-animal-rights/.

of profiling and spying on activist and community organizations, from Black Panthers and women's right activists, to food co-op members and bike repair collectives as part of anti-Communist sentiments informed by the Cold War politics of the 60s, 70s, and 80s. The Portland Police spent more time spying on people who practiced leftist politics than uncovering, or stopping, any violent "terrorist" activity.[26] About the surveillance and police harassment, Kent Ford, the head of the now-defunct Black Panther Party in Portland said, "'Economically and financially, they just about destroyed me."[27] More recently, in 2019, the Joint Terrorism Task Force, and other similar organizations throughout Oregon, were revealed to be monitoring climate, Native American, and anti-oil pipeline activists.[28] However, while white supremacist militias and anti-abortion groups had long been active in the Pacific Northwest (and throughout the country), they did not operate under the same level of surveillance or media scrutiny. In 2005 Vermont Senator James Jeffords pointed out that, "The Department of Homeland Security needs to protect us from all terrorist threats, and should not focus on eco-terrorism at the expense of other domestic terrorist groups, such as the KKK, right wing militias, abortion clinic bombers, and skin heads."[29] Ecoterrorism, and leftist activism that employed creative, direct

26 Ben Jacklet, *The Secret Watchers*, The Portland Tribune, September 12, 2002, pamplinmedia.com/component/content/article?id=117580. Accessed on March 10, 2020.

27 Ibid.

28 Jason Wilson and Will Parish, *Revealed: FBI and police monitoring Oregon anti-pipeline activists*, The Guardian, August 8, 2019, theguardian.com/us-news/2019/aug/08/fbi-oregon-anti-pipeline-jordan-cove-activists. Accessed March 10, 2020.

29 "ECO-TERRORISM SPECIFICALLY EXAMINING THE EARTH LIBERATION FRONT AND ANIMAL LIBERATION FRONT," Hearing before the Committee on Environment and Public Works, 109th Congress, First Sesseion, May 18, 2005. Available at: govinfo.gov/content/pkg/CHRG-109shrg32209/html/CHRG-109shrg32209.htm Accessed on January 5, 2021.

action tactics in general, had become a particular focus for the police and FBI in the late 1990s and early 2000s.

Knowing we were under potential FBI scrutiny as budding activists gave us an exaggerated sense of our own self-importance. Deirdre drew connections between possible surveillance of our group to surveillance of Black Power groups in the 60s and 70s, trying to push us to be as radical in our scope and vision. It felt absurd to expect that our group of young women could operate on such a level, especially because we had such varying levels of political consciousness and experience, though given the Portland Police's history of spying on activists it wasn't out of the question. However, to put our group in the same category of the Black Panthers was an act of appropriation and fetishizing our idea of the Panthers, as opposed to the political reality. We also didn't take into account the amount of police surveillance and racial profiling that communities of color, in Portland and beyond, faced every day, whether they identified as activists or not. This kind of systemic racism continues, and nearly 20 years later, in 2019 a study of police stops in Oregon found that after a traffic stop in Portland, 11 percent of Black drivers faced a search, more than double the predicted rate of 4.8 percent.[30] In recounting a police raid of her home in Los Angeles in 2012, Patrisse Khan-Cullors, co-founder of the Black Lives Matter movement, reflects on the long history of surveillance, harassment, terrorism, and violence faced by Black communities by law enforcement. She writes, "Another story that does not get told when they tell the

30 Conrad Wilson, "Oregon Traffic Stop Data Shows Largest Disparity At Portland, Hillsboro Police," Oregon Public Broadcasting, 12/1/2019, opb.org/news/article/oregon-portland-traffic-stop-data-disparity-portland-hillsboro/ accessed on 1/5/2021.

story of California is the story of occupation, of what it means for so many of us who are Black or Latinx to live unable to escape the constant monitoring by police, the idea that your very existence, the brown of your skin, is enough to get you snatched up, enough to get you killed."[31] While our group often talked about wanting to fight systemic racism, by conflating the kind of scrutiny we might be under from law enforcement to what Black activists and community members had experienced in Portland for decades placed ourselves at the center of a narrative that was not ours to claim. This reflected both our own privilege, naitivite, and as people mostly new to Portland, disconnection from the politics outside of punk feminism and anarchism that impacted the place where we had chosen to live.

As we planned our first collective action we tried to puzzle out how to embrace direct action like the ELF while also creating a space for ourselves to explore our identities as feminist artists and expand the idea of what kind of action could be considered radical. All around Portland, new residents from California who worked in the tech sector were buying and renovating classic Northwest bungalow houses. They were part of an influx of new residents to the city that averaged about 10,000 a year.[32] Monthly art walks highlighted the new galleries and restaurants in immigrant and formerly industrial neighborhoods that had recently been considered too dangerous for middle class white people. Gentrification, a word many of us had just learned, would be the target of our first action. We decided to wheat paste

31 Patrisse Khan-Cullors and Asha Bandele, "When They Call You a Terrorist," New York: St. Martin's Griffin, 2017,p. 185.
32 Portland Population, worldpopulationreview.com/us-cities/portland/ accessed on 10/10/2019.

posters with radical slogans like "Art and revolution go hand and hand!" and "Art is not for sale!" in wealthier neighborhoods. As we prepared for our first actions, we didn't fully realize how, as punks and artists living in low-rent neighborhoods, many of us arrived from wealthier, coastal metropolitan areas and were also contributing to gentrification.

As the majority of us pasted our ransom-note style posters around town in pairs, sticking them to telephone poles, trash cans, and newspaper boxes, Deirdre slipped off on her own. Later, she admitted to me she had been pasting the posters directly on SUVs. When it dried, the wheat paste would be impossible to remove without ruining the vehicle's paint job. I felt stung that Deirdre had left me out of her more radical plan, but was conflicted. Could making the choice to ruin the paint job of a few individual SUVs help make the case for the power of feminist art, critique gentrification, or sound the alarm about the dangers of global capitalism? Were we just privileged, petty vandals? As a majority white group, what would have happened if we got caught? Irresponsibly, we'd hardly discussed it as a possibility. While we thought we were committing a radical act of public art and education, we were also serving to prop up our own radical self-image.

This kind of disconnect between political priorities and orientations was not uncommon in other feminist groups. In Riot Grrrl chapters in the early 1990s there had been intense debates about the central purpose of the groups. Were they more personal—an intimate place for young women to share and center on their stories and experiences, connect with each other, and create "revolution in their everyday lives" as the Riot Grrrl manifesto proposed? Or were Riot Grrrls supposed to be publically political—such as having a radical, disruptive presence at pro-choice rallies and marches, or to actively confront men in bands who were identified as perpetuators of abusive behavior torwards women? Groups had splintered over differences in their answers to these questions, leading to a fractured movement, something we were hoping to alleviate and overcome in our art collective, though we didn't have a plan for this—we hoped that being conscious of past activism groups' challenges and our own enthusiasm would be enough to magically sustain us.

In Portland's microcosm, issues like gentrification felt like something immediate that we could both impact and attempt to control. George W. Bush's looming inauguration in January of 2001 stirred a bout of collective dread and served as a harsh reminder of the larger political reality that existed beyond our self-constructed girl utopia. In a warning sign of presidential elections to come in 2004 and 2016, Bush lost the popular vote by 50,456,002 votes to Al Gore's 50,999,897, but still became the president thanks to the electoral college and a Supreme Court decision that ended a controversial vote recount in Florida.

Despite the fact I'd spent my high school activist years battling regressive anti-LGBTQ and anti-abortion bills in my home state of Maine, before the election I'd held out hope that an expansive political vision that centered expanding rights for women, people of color, and LGBTQ people would gain cultural and political traction. This ignored the fact that throughout the 1990s conservatism had been steadily gaining momentum, similar to how conservatives continued to consolidate power and shape the cultural conversation throughout the Obama administration. Republicans had won the majority of seats in the House of Representatives in 1994. Conservative politics found a mainstream voice with the launch of news outlets like Fox News in 1996 and the Drudge Report in 1997. The Republicans had extremely effective ways to mobilize voters, spread their interpretation of the news, and control local elections. However, similar to the election that would play out in 2016, the presidential victory of a buffoon-like candidate such as George W. Bush felt like a slap in the face of my budding feminist politics.

All fall the news had been full of reports of gerrymandered districts, questions about the accuracy of voting machines due to new technology, and shifting polling places and voting policies in Southern and Midwestern states. This made it more difficult for communities of color and senior citizens to vote, and gave Republican candidates the electoral advantage. These kinds of news stories would become the backdrop to every major election that followed through the Bush, Obama, and Trump years and point to how Republicans responded to a diminishing power base by consolidating their power through voter suppression. However, the punk and radical communities in Portland and beyond regarded this kind of cynical maneuvering as par for the course. Instead of seeing these kinds of policies as indicative of the kind of systemic oppression we were committed to ending, my friends harbored attitudes that ranged from mistrust to outright disdain for mainstream, electoral politics, even when the issues deeply affected us. The prevailing belief, especially by those who identified loosely as anarchists, was that everyone in government was a crony in the service of exploitative capitalism, so what did it matter what party they were part of? Unfortunately, this also increased our sense of powerlessness and gave our activism a kind of "all or nothing feel"—either you brought on the revolution or you didn't—instead of recognizing political change as a spectrum and a constantly evolving practice.

On the day of Bush's inauguration in 2001 an estimated 20,000 people protested in Washington DC. While this would later be dwarfed by the estimated 200,000 who protested in DC and over 5 million people throughout the US who participated in the Women's March in 2017 to protest Trump's inauguration,[33] the protests against Bush were the first time there had been major protests of a presidential inauguration since Nixon took office for the second time in 1973.[34] Portland felt very far from any center of political power, though a range of local activist groups were represented at the protest: labor organizers, environmentalists, black bloc anarchists, LGBTQ groups, and the requisite large papier mache puppets. Our anti-Bush chants bounced off the buildings surrounding the park where the protest was held, turning it into an echo chamber.

Third-wave feminism was predicated upon the belief in the importance of women's individual experiences and our power to challenge sexist oppression on multiple levels, but it was not always clear how to translate that into political power. Public, visible resistance through protest was important, but it needed to

---

33 Wikipedia, "2017 Women's March," accessed October 14, 2019, en.wikipedia.org/wiki/2017_Women%27s_March.

34 David E. Rosenbaum, "The Inauguration: The Demonstrations," The New York Times, January 21, 2001, accessed on October 8, 2019, nytimes.com/2001/01/21/us/inauguration-demonstrations-protesters-thousands-sound-off-capital.html.

be coupled with strategy, community connections, and tangible results to be sustainable. We learn about how to balance our values, ideals, and actions through trial and error, but in my late teens, like many young activists, I was looking for a revolutionary blueprint and leader to follow.

There had long been tensions in punk and Riot Grrrl subcultures about the place of explicit activism—some taking part because they were more interested in and motivated by the friendships, music, and sense of belonging as opposed to explicit protest. The punk community in the late 1990s and early 2000s was committed to the "do it yourself" ethos, and much activism focused on taking a self-empowered approach to politics in your life, similar to the Riot Grrrl manifesto's encouragement to create revolution in our daily lives. These included eating vegan, riding a bike instead of driving, exploring alternative medicine and natural remedies, and reflecting on how your privilege and identity informed your life and then self-publishing a zine or online journal about it. However, how to take a DIY approach to global politics and systemic oppression was less clear, especially because being part of a movement and movement building was a much longer, more indirect process.

The tension between what constituted personal consciousness and political change, and where the focus should be, played out in our art collective. Several of us formed a splinter group to organize a small protest against Bush's reinstation of the "global gag rule," which prevented US international aid money to be given to healthcare facilities that provided abortion abroad, beacuse some members didn't feel comfortable "endorsing" certain political actions. Due to this, some members felt betrayed because they wanted to focus more on making art and felt judged for not being "radical" enough. Tensions had also been rising between the white women in the collective and the women of color. Collective members of color rightly pointed out that white women could not fully understand their experience no matter how "anti-racist" they were, fueling resent from some of the white women. This phenomenon, which has been summarized (and meme-ified) as "white tears" meant white women's hurt feelings and egos stayed at the center of the conversations, instead of prioritizing and listening to the experiences and ideas of women of color. It also meant that the burden to educate white women about what racism looked like and how it operated fell unduly on the women of color in the group. In many ways, instead of committing to grow politically and be accountable to each other while understanding our roles in society, many of the white group members wanted to be right, rather than of trying to do better by each other and the radical values we professed to share.

Similar tensions had erupted throughout the Riot Grrrl movement and pulled those groups apart. Fallouts due to race and class differences that took place at Riot Grrrl meetings and conventions throughout the 1990s were well documented in zines. A zinester named Sisi wrote about how conversations about race tended to happen only after, not during, the Riot Grrrl meetings she attended in Los Angeles in the mid-1990s, to avoid tension with the majority-white group. "It's easier for white wimmin and girls to ignore these issues," she wrote in *Evolution of a Race Riot*, "because they are surrounded by others like them and don't have to feel out of place because of their color, language, religion and traditions ... unless there is a disparity in their financial situation."[35] Knowing about this past history did not help our group avoid similar tensions. In the feminist art collective we became hyper vigilant, calling each other "on our shit" despite the fact none of us were experts or experienced activists or facilitators, and many of us were encourntering political activism for the first time. Often these callouts took the form of emails or online messages, adding to the weight of what was not addressed in person and silence and tension in the group.

It was important to recognize the weight of what later would be called "emotional labor" that was often undertaken by women and people of color who were involved in art and social change. However, at the time, for many radicals "activism" still seemed to translate into anti-globalization street protest and direct action, like those undertaken by the ELF, not a nuanced understanding of the complex and long term work it took to organize and build liberatory communities and movements. With the rise of another generation of young activists there now is a broader range of entry points for political involvement, but tensions around what "real" activism looks like remain. Similar to the tensions in our group, those who build community and awareness online, via letter writing and text message campaigns, or through doing administrative volunteer work are often labeled as "armchair" activists, despite the vital work they do. Instead of looking at how different talents and strengths can help support robust

35 Sisi (Housewife Turned Assassin) in *Evolution of a Race Riot*, Mini Nguyen ed. Berkely, CA: Self-published, 1997, 52.

movements, pointing fingers at who is a more committed activist or feminist fractures movements and shuts down vital discussion.

While the third wave feminists, Riot Grrrls, punks, and activists, such as ourselves, didn't always recognize it, the call out culture and protection of personal ego that had become part of these scenes echoed challenges that had been a part of feminist organizing for decades. Second Wave feminists referred to it as "trashing." In an article entitled "Trashing: The Dark Side of Sisterhood" published in *Ms.* in 1976, Jo Freeman recounts her experiences being "trashed" in the 1960s and 70s women's movement. In it she defines "trashing" not as healthy conflict or disagreement, but "a particularly vicious form of character assassination... It is manipulative, dishonest, and excessive. ... It is not done to expose disagreements or resolve differences. It is done to disparage and destroy."[36] These experiences also foreshadowed the even more vicious and public call out culture that would be amplified through social media platforms such as Twitter in the coming decades.

In response to toxic "call out" culture in the mid-2010's, activists developed strategies for "calling in"—a more compassionate, empathetic response to oppressive behavior within social justice movements. While imperfect, the simple acknowledgement that people with good intentions make mistakes and can learn from their behavior represents an important shift. Another key aspect of "calling in" is that it does not expect those who occupy oppressed positions to take on the job of educating those

---

36 Jo Freeman, original published in Ms. April 1976, pp. 49-51, 92-98. Accessed at: jofreeman.com/joreen/trashing.htm

in positions of power about their own privilege. While greater resources now exist for activists to address ostracizing behavior within their circles, it takes self-awareness and a long term perspective on the process of social justice and social change to invest in transforming harmful behaviors and parsing out where there is potential for growth and change and how to encourage this without falling into activist burnout.

For feminists looking for their version of utopia, instead of enforcing rigid perfection, we need to cultivate spaces for growth and accountability. We need to take ownership of our mistakes. We need to learn about who has come before us and about organizing that is happening in communities beyond our own. We need to trust we are building on and contributing to generations of political organizing even though it's not always clear how in the moment. It's both frustrating and comforting to know we can't even know everything about feminism, social change, or each other, but by working for it we can create pockets of practical utopia. Our striving realities are less cozy than an isolated girl utopia, but more attainable as we grow and continue to nurture our revolutionary spark.

Feminist utopia, or utopia of any kind, is not a place you can find on a map. Building it is not as simple as bringing together a group of fellow feminists, and trusting a charismatic leader to show the way. Becoming a feminist activist is not as simple as engaging in the "right" kinds of public actions, though it's important to try, knowing you will make mistakes along the way. In addition, people do not get involved in feminism or political groups only for politics—there are more complex forces at play. Sara Marucs reflection on this in *Girls to the Front*, writing, "People join political cultures or subcultures for a combination of reasons. To feel righteous, to feel less helpless, to distance ourselves from a dominant culture that repels us, to feel like we have a purpose, to make friends, to find love or sex, to relive the way you once felt when a certain song swept thorugh you at a rally or coffeehouse or club or basement and aligned all the molecules in your body."[37] Our radical art collective came together, and fell apart, for many of the reasons Marcus describes. We did not realize that we, like all activists, had to embrace an inherent tension: understanding politics and the world as it is and envisioning and working for a world as it could be. We had wanted to skip ahead to where we already knew ourselves and knew how to make art and revolution together. We tried to force, instead of grow, a spirit of cooperation and collaboration. Inherent to being political people is the fact that we will mess up and treat people badly, and we are always still learning and growing as activists and people—a process which is never complete. Part of this process is owning our shortcomings and acknowledging what we don't already know.

Feminism is not an identity that can shelter us from the mess and oppressions of the world, but an expansive political practice that can help us develop tools to confront it. I believe an important part of our work as feminists is not to find or create a "girl utopia" that is isolated from the rest of the world, but instead to carve out a place in our current, imperfect reality where we can ground ourselves and work with others to reach for collective change.

---

37 Sara Marcus, *Girls to the Front*, New York: Harper Perennial, 2010, 320.

PART TWO

FORGING
FEMINIST
COMMUNITY

A BOSTON MARRIAGE
Embracing the radical possibility of feminist friendship

"You say we are 'out to kill the white boy mentality,' but have you examined your own mentality?"

"Your white, upper middle class girl mentality? What if I said I wanted to kill that mentality too?"

That's me, I thought. Who was this zine writer who spoke so clearly and boldly about issues that so many in my white, middle class family and high school refused to talk about?

The author, Lauren, went on to explain how she was Chinese, Jewish, and queer. Born and raised in New York City, she wrote about seeing shows at iconic downtown punk clubs like Coney Island High and Meow Mix and going to Riot Grrrl meetings on the Lower East Side. Hailing from the hayfields and sleepy coastal towns of Maine, as I read I couldn't help but yearn for her life. She also wrote about the frustration of growing up on Staten Island, isolated from the cool things happening in Manhattan and Brooklyn, and how she felt like the only one of her kind in her giant, public high school. What she described felt like my own life, even if there were vast differences between us.

She had a direct quality to her writing, along with a thoughtfulness, deep critical analysis, and a subtle, dry sense of humor. Her zines provided me with a road map of what the transition from high school Riot Grrrl to intellectual, radical college-bound feminist could look like. When we finally met, she looked like the hand drawn self-portraits from her zine: short, thick, black hair; dark framed glasses; clad in a thrifted button-down shirt, jeans, and Puma sneakers. I wasn't sure what she might see in me as a pink-haired, high school aspiring Riot Grrrl, but I felt the spark of possibility that we could be real life friends. As a greeting, she presented me with a silk-screened patch she had just made: a drawing of a studded bracelet with the words "punk rock expatriate" around it.

"It's about how I became disillusioned by the whiteness of punk rock," she explained, "And felt like I outgrew punk, even if I still believe in some of the do-it-yourself ideals." The idea of being a "punk rock expatriate" seemed to open a world of possibility of different ways to approach activism, art, and life.

In the early-to-mid 2000s there was a network of women whose ages spanned from our late teens to early thirties whose lives had been changed by discovering Riot Grrrl and zines. In these zines we untangled our web of identities; discussed power, privilege, and favorite books and bands; and often referenced sleep overs, hangouts, and get togethers where we met each other. Even though they spanned geographies, these friendships, nurtured through letters, AOL instant messenger, and later Livejournal, were immediate, consuming, and necessary. They were also grounded in feminism and the Riot Grrrl idea that being loving and supportive of other women is an explicit tactic to resist the patriarchy and sexist competition for men's affection. Being part of this network felt distinctly separate from a macho tradition of punk and one that was more expansive.

In the early 2000s, Lauren and I moved in together soon after I moved to New York City in a sagging apartment building in South

Brooklyn. Like many young women in their twenties, it felt like we were living lives that were usually reserved for couples, but we were forging ahead with each other and subverting the narrative that a woman was only grown up when she moved in with (and married) a man. As a nod to our punk and Riot Grrrl past, I sewed a flag with a skull and crossbones with a bow on top of it and the words "GIRL PIRATE" below and hung it in our entryway. I had come there not only for college, but like most young people who come to New York: because it offered opportunities for cultural discovery, political consciousness, and personal transformation beyond what was on offer at home. Throughout history, cities have always offered more space than rural areas for young women to pursue their education, creative practice, and career, and explore who they are beyond the domestic sphere. Indeed, demographically young single women are more concentrated in urban areas.[38]

In her 2016 book *All The Single Ladies* Rebecca Traister explored the importance of female friendships in shaping women's identities, dreams, and goals, writing, "Among the largely unacknowledged truth of female life is that women's primary, foundational, formative relationships are as likely to be with each other as they are with the men we've been told since childhood are supposed to be the people who complete us."[39] However, in the early 2000s there was little cultural acknowledgement that the relationships young women were forming could be the defining relationship of their twenties and beyond. There was one pop culture touchstone: Carrie Bradshaw and her privileged

38 citylab.com/equity/2015/02/where-in-the-us-are-there-more-single-men-than-women/385369
39 Rebecca Traister, *All The Single Ladies*, New York: Simon and Schuster, 2016, 97.

band of brunchers. Despite the women's friendships *Sex in the City* portrayed, in many ways, the show reinforced a dyanmic that despite our friendships, we were still expected to pursue men as our focus and marriage and children as our goal. There were few social traditions to recognize and appreciate the importance we played in each other's lives.

Riot Grrrl had idolized adolescent versions of girl friendship, and punk in general privileged the idea of a "scene" or crew of friends over individualized romantic relationships. For many women in their twenties, thirties, and beyond, this continues to be the case, with friends relying on each other to navigate both the significant and mundane events of adulthoods: birthdays, new jobs and layoffs, fresh crushes and hard breakups, and coping with aging and dying and parents. About this phenomenon journalist Jill Filipovic writes, "[E]ven though friendships between women are pervasive, definitional, and life sustaining, there's often little recognition of them. There are no anniversaries or milestones to celebrate, not even an assumption or understanding that friendships often outshine romantic relationships."[40] Feminists and queer women inspired by Riot Grrrl and Third Wave feminism knew it was up to us to build our own lives, not wait for someone else to define our lives for us. To paraphrase Gloria Steinem, we were on our way to becoming the "men we wanted to marry" and in many ways, serving that role for each other.

For many, feminist friendships are also a chance to more deeply explore lived feminist politics. Feminism is important to center as a practice, because simply being involved in punk subculture or

40 Jill Filipovic, *The H-Spot: The Feminist Pursuit of Happiness*, New York: Nation Books, 2017, 40.

supporting other women does not automatically contribute to a deeply lived, anti-oppressive feminist practice. For example, there were many other radical women writing zines, but some of them seemed more focused on establishing themselves as punk rock cool in the eyes of men, one going so far as to proclaim herself an "anti-girl girl." Friendships organized around the principles of feminism resist this kind of competitive individualism, as well as the heteronormative-sanctioned "girlfriendships" celebrated by stereotypical sorority sisters and at bachelorette parties. They include a willingness to think critically about how social privilege and power function in society and within the relationship. In the words of Filipovic, "Friendships make us happier, and they can also make us more radical."[41] A feminist friendship also serves as a mechanism for actively discovering and supporting other feminists. For Lauren and I this included attending feminist performances, art exhibits, and protests together and helping each other discover radical, queer feminist artists and writers.

Women born in the 70s and 80s are part of a demographic trend where women, especially those with a college education, are delaying or outright rejecting marriage. The average age of marriage in the US has risen to 27 for women and 29 for men.[42] Personally, Lauren and I embraced and celebrated the idea of the spinster, of the woman solo by choice and in possession of her power, though friends and family were sometimes shocked and bemused that we, as young women, would use the term to refer to ourselves. Their reaction was a reminder that an independent

41 Ibid, 41.
42 pewresearch.org/fact-tank/2017/09/14/as-u-s-marriage-rate-hovers-at-50-education-gap-in-marital-status-widens/

woman, especially one who revels in her independence, could still be a contentious cultural phenomenon, even in the new millennium.

In her book *Spinster*, Kate Bolick remarks that the image of the spinster, originally a positive reference to independent, employed women who spun thread in the 19th century, is a "lightning rod for attitudes towards women in general." Bolick observes that "in spite of her prevalence the single woman is nearly always considered an anomaly, an aberration from the social order."[43] Going farther than Bolick, Briallen Hopper reminds her readers of the radical past and present of the spinster, writing, ""[The spinster] is often weird, difficult, dissonant and queer ... And her social and emotional life is not primarily oriented around the familiar forms of straight romance."[44] Hopper emphasizes that spinsters, and others who fall outside of traditional heterosexual partnership, have the chance to forge powerful friendships and build communities defined by their values and ideals. Close friendships and partnerships between women have also been called "Boston Marriages," which is drawn from the late-19th and early-20th centuries to describe a committed partnership between two women who live together free of financial support from a man. Certainly, there's a proud tradition of dynamic, historic friendships between women that have moved art, politics, and culture forward. About the impact of friendships like this, Rebecca Traister wrote, "... women find themselves growing into themselves, shaping their identities, dreams and goals not

43 Kate Bolick, *Spinster: Making a Life of One's Own*, New York: Crown Publishers, 2015, 15.
44 Briallen Hopper, *Hard to Love*, New York: Bloomsbury Publishing, 2019, 42.

necessarily in tandem with a man or within a traditional family structure, but instead alongside other women. Their friends."[45]

Multiple studies have shown that women's friendships are not only formative and emotionally fulfilling, but also deliver long-term health benefits, making those who tend to friendships and have strong communities less likely to develop physical ailments and more resilient when it comes to handling trauma and stress,[46] meaning that we also have many reasons to continue to nurture these friendships as our lives evolve. In *The H-Spot*, Jill Filipovic speaks to this phenomenon. She writes, "There's an expectation— often born out—that women's friendships will recede once they're replaced by the more valid, real, and recognized romantic relationships. There's also no road map for them, especially as women age out of their twenties."[47]

As women get older, their friend groups shift, and certainly in a heterosexist, capitalist patriarchy there are few models for feminist friendship, and the Riot Grrrl ideal of grrrl love before everything else can be difficult to hold onto as adult life becomes more complex. Participation in a girl-oriented feminist subculture doesn't necessarily fully translate into ambitions of serious careers, couplehood, and/or riasing children. This was certainly the case for Lauren and my friendship, along with others in our friendship group, and while our bonds were still strong, it was hard to maintain the same level of intensity as careers, studies, and partnerships took us in different directions emotionally and eventually to different cities. Change in friendships is

45 Traister, 97.
46 huffingtonpost.com/randy-kamen-gredinger-edd/female-friendship_b_2193062.html
47 Filipovic, 40.

inevitable, as Kayleen Shaefer explains, "It's impossible to keep our friendships static … We move, get new jobs, fall in love, or give birth, and sometimes there isn't going to be a way to equalize everyone in our lives, whether the imbalance comes from logistical or emotional upheaval, or some combination of both."[48] However, many women who formed close bonds through feminist subcutlures were both searching for who we could become and how we could move our youthful, Riot Grrrl ideals forward as adults. While women are often instructed that romantic relationships take work in order to work through differences and difficulties, we rarely are instructed to give our friendships the same level of energy and care, especially as our lives change. Often we believe friendships simply happened instead of being built through deliberate, careful choices. If we took time to articulate to ourselves and each other the centrality our friendships play in our lives and acknowledge the energy they take to sustain, we could be in a better position to enable them to evolve consciously and healthily.

Recently, intimate friendships between women have been more widely recognized and celebrated in popular culture, from the growing popularity of the Valentine's Day alternative Galentine's Day, to the *Broad City* television series, to books like *Work Wife*, movies like *Girl's Trip*, and the *Call Your Girlfriend* podcast. Alex Smith explores in *The Guardian* why friendships between women are such a potent subject for creative work: "Female friendship, with its additional charge of possible subversion – a world free from male control—is densely suggestive... it raises knotty

48 Kayleen Schaefer, *Text Me When You Get Home*, New York: Dutton, 2018, 221.

questions of the individual's ability to disrupt gender norms as well as her often unconscious adherence to them."[49] In service to this complexity, as well as an expansive interpretation of feminism that continuously questions gender norms, we need to avoid emotionally-and-politically bankrupt "you go girl" platitudes that ignore how power informs women's relationships. We should be cautious of those who celebrate their "girl squads" while failing to acknowledge their own economic, heterosexual, and racial privilege, such as that invoked by Taylor Swift's "squad goals" (epitomized by her 2015 video for *Bad Blood* where she strutted around with other rich and famous women), Lana Del Rey, or Lena Dunham.

To take a radical, feminist approach to celebrating friendships between women means centering many different modes of friendship, family, romance, and the possibility of building one's life outside of traditional, heterosexual structures. Writer Sadie Graham pointed out that American culture's recent focus on women's friendships often centers heterosxual women and leaves the experience of queer women out. She writes, "It might help us recognize how when straightness is the assumed default, gestures of queer intimacy get muddled, blurred, and erased amidst all that platonic friendships have been stretched to encompass."[50] Centering our friendships just as much, or more than, our romantic relationships is a gesture that can disrupt heterosexual, patriarchal culture, but only if we stay critical of

---

49 theguardian.com/books/2016/aug/06/women-friendship-wold-ferrante-zadie-smith-fiction-alex-clark
50 Sadie Graham, "How Our Cultural Obsession with 'Girlfriendship' Sidelines Queer Women," *Vice*, published August 6, 2018, vice.com/en_us/article/wjk45z/straight-girlfriends-queer-women.

the power structures in which these relationships exist and build power together.

There is an expectation that as people couple up they place their partner at the center of their social world and if they have kids, their social lives shift again to focus on friends with children. As Kayleen Schaefer notes, "Prioritizing friendship is sometimes tricky; society often indicates to women that it's not on the same level as the other relationships in our lives, such as the ones with our romantic partners, our children, or even our jobs."[51] What does adult friendship look like when you want to keep cultivating an emotional depth and expansiveness, while you also know you have other obligations on your time and emotional energy? How do you keep those friendships centered on political values of equality, liberation, and expansive vision of the future? The first step is making a conscious decision to do so.

Many in radical and queer circles has pioneered the idea of building "alternative," "chosen," or "found" families and extended, caring networks of friends. This idea acknowledges that deep friendships are incredibly important and life sustaining. This concept can be extended to think about how our friendships can be radical and transformative, and rethink structures of caring that go beyond traditional couple relationships and families. Briallen Hopper acknowledges this, writing, "… as a spinster who craves connection and community above all and who has found it outside of the standard couple form, I've come to realize that I owe an immeasurable debt to the intersecting groups of people who have historically been barred from the privileges of marriage

51 Kayleen Schaefer, *Text Me When You Get Home*, New York: Dutton, 2018, 118.

by law and demography and have learned to create intimate lives apart from it. In other words, I'm indebted to queer people and to African Americans."[52] She goes on to point out that traditional marriage as it has been defined and promoted in the United States fails to recognize and protect families who are pathologized and torn apart by incarceration, deportation, and national borders. Connecting our feminist friendships to the fight for equality is a strategy for not only centering different types of relationships in our lives, but creating cultural change.

The radical friendships formed through Riot Grrrl, punk, and zines helped an extended network of women, radicals, and queer people feel we were part of a larger movement while conveying a sense of intimate closeness with each other. The ideas we nurtured not only pushed us to protect, support, and encourage each other, but envision and fight for a more expansive world. While it may not look like the scrawled manifestos in zines, punk shows, and sleepovers of our late teens or the potlucks, game nights, and sprawling collective hangouts of our mid-twenties, as feminists we need to carry forward that feeling as we envision the next part of our lives. Now, we would do well to consider practically how the "spinster dream" or "Boston Marriages" of our twenties, of imagining ourselves living together when we are retired and taking care of gardens and cats, could become the lived reality of our 70s and 80s.

Feminist friendships can be a major disruption of our current social structure. They can resist the idea of the heterosexual couple as an organizing principal of our lives and as the

---

52 Hopper, 53.

fundamental building block of society. As such, as we nurture our friendships we also have a responsibility to collectively imagine what our future could look like beyond our individual friendships and friend groups. How can we assure our collective future beyond reliance on state-sanctioned matrimony and the traditional family structure? We should continue to ask ourselves what a feminist approach to community, aging, and caretaking can look like on a policy and societal level and fight for a vision that doesn't rely on being in a couple to access a full range of benefits and a secure future.

Deep care, listening, support, and political activism between women, especially those of different backgrounds, takes time and can be painful. But when we no longer take our feminist friendships for granted they can continue to shake the foundations of a sexist society that positioned the heterosexual family as the ultimate model of adulthood. This is something my friendship with Lauren taught me and continues to teach me. Feminist friendship doesn't mean friendship at all costs, but that we continue to invest in the women who have played a key role in our lives. Nurturing feminist friendships also means working for a society that supports all different configurations of relationships and one that centers care, empathy, and equality. When our friendships nurture our activism, we can also nurture them. With radical honesty and flexibility, our friendships can and will continue to radically reshape all phases of our lives and the society we live them in.

REWRITING THE MARRIAGE PLOT: MOVING BEYOND THE WEDDING-INDUSTRIAL COMPLEX

"**I**f you can, marry a rich man," my mother told me once when I was about nine years old. "Money isn't everything, but it helps."

"I am never getting married," I responded, looking back at her steadily.

Like other ideas we inherit from our culture, ideals about partnership and marriage infuse our sense of identity and self long before we are conscious about how they are shaping our beliefs, values, ambitions, and dreams. During the 1980s when I was a child *People* magazine reported breathlessly on the fairytale, and fallout, of the wedding of Princess Diana, inspiring a generation of copycat dresses. As white, middle class, educated women pushed to achieve more at work and to "break the glass ceiling" in the business world, these single, career-driven women were also a spectre to be feared and mocked as cold, bitchy, and unlovable. In parallel, weddings became the center of what a young woman should dream about and aspire to as the best day of her life.

Through Riot Grrrl zines, feminists were able to connect with other young women's stories about their parents' dysfunctional relationships, as well as the violence and emotional manipulation some of the authors had experienced at the hands of their partners. Riot Grrrl was about declaring an end to sexist oppression on an intimate level. It also pushed the women who were involved to analyze how patriarchy and sexism seeped into the intimate spaces in our personal lives and relationships. Of course it was also nuanced: girls in the punk and Riot Grrrl subcultures had crushes and competed for the attention of boys and each other, and these kind of interpersonal tensions caused more than a little strain to the Riot Grrrl adage, "Jealousy kills grrrl love."

Marriage has long been a contentious subject within many different generations of the feminist movements. In *Manifesta*, one of the defining works of Third Wave feminism (published in 2000), authors Jennifer Baumgardner and Amy Richards tried to bring light to the debate on marriage, asking, "In an odd paradox, why do many feminists today have to justify why they are single and why they get married?"[53] The authors list reasons that still ring true: fulfilling romantic dreams, access to health care and tax benefits, to raise children, to find comfort and companionship, and to please their families, among thousands of others. What the authors fail to bring up, however, is that none of these "choices" is neutral and they are influenced not only by patriarchal cultural tradition, but by capitalism. In the United States in 2019 the wedding industry was worth an approximate 76 billion dollars.[54] While there may be many roads that lead to marriage and long term commitment to a romantic partner, the choice to marry and to have a wedding is not a neutral one.

The institution of marriage is a clear power structure that reinforced sexism, gendered divisions of labor, and ossified notions of love, family, and care. Weddings, the popular culture

53 Jennifer Baumgardner and Amy Richards, *Manifesta: Young Women, Feminism, and the Future* (New York: Farrar, Straus and Giroux, 2010), 39.

54 IbisWorld, "Wedding Services Industry in the US," accessed on October 22, 2019, ibisworld.com/united-states/market-research-reports/wedding-services-industry/.

narrative goes, are singular moments of self-transformation and a crowning achievement in a couple's life together. When wedding invitations started arriving in batches in my late twenties and early thirties I found the fairytale of a wedding and the achievement it represented hard to resist, even as the ceremonies and celebrations themselves tended to blur together into a sea of navigating mud puddles in high heels at wedding farms, mason jar cocktails, artisanal cheese plates, calligraphy place cards, and overpriced hotel rooms and rental cars. My experience with these weddings was a reminder of the depth that the idea of a monogamous, often heterosexual, marriage as an aspirational ideal is deeply socialized into our consciousness, as well as ingrained in American culture, even for those of us who have spent time in anti-authoritarian and anti-institutional subcultures like punk. It is also a reminder of how contemporary feminists must continue to push to reimagine and rebuild structures of care and access to cultural power in a way that is not dependent upon the family or the couple.

Many millennials represent an overall trend in the United States: delaying marriage or not marrying at all. As reported by Pew in 2016, the median age of marriage for women is 27 and for men is 29, up from 23 for women and 26 for men in 1990.[55] Often, people are taking the time to pursue education and build their careers before they get married. In addition, as of 2012, one fifth of Americans had never been married, down from one tenth in 1960, and many people are living together and having children

55 Kim Parker and Renee Stepler, "As U.S. marriage rate hovers at 50%, education gap in marital status widens," published September 14, 2017, accessed on June 28, 2018. pewresearch.org/fact-tank/2017/09/14/as-u-s-marriage-rate-hovers-at-50-education-gap-in-marital-status-widens/

outside of "traditional" marriage.[56] These statistics also represent a growing "marriage gap," as class and marital status are more closely linked than ever before. Concisely put, those with greater education and economic and social privilege are more likely to be married, and marriage rates vary widely by ethnicity. For example, 54% of white adults were married, compared to 46% of black adults.[57] Middle class women in particular have benefitted in terms of higher salaries and lifetime earning from "delaying" marriage. As journalist Rebecca Traister explores in her book *All The Single Ladies*, couples from upper middle class backgrounds now have more money to spend and, when they do get married, it's often to show off their own professional achievements and unique taste.

Marriage for middle class women is no longer a fairytale where a woman passively waits for her prince (or princess). It is now positioned as a mark of professional achievement, a performance of adulthood, and the ultimate expression of individual choice. This stands in stark relief from the way marriage had been pushed on low-income, single women and couples of color during the Bush-era as a "poverty reduction" strategy that largely failed.[58] In an interview with Jezebel, Rebecca Traister explained, "...Marriage is no longer the thing that kicks off a woman's adult life. As sociologists put it, marriage is now a capstone event instead ... Marriage is popularly a sign that your life is in

---

56 Wendy Wang and Kim Parker, "Record share of Americans have never married," published September 24, 2014, accessed on October 22, 2019, pewsocialtrends.org/2014/09/24/record-share-of-americans-have-never-married/.

57 Parker and Stepler, pewresearch.org/fact-tank/2017/09/14/as-u-s-marriage-rate-hovers-at-50-education-gap-in-marital-status-widens/

58 Stephanie Mencimer, "The GOP's Dead-End Marriage Program," *Mother Jones*, published June 25, 2012, accessed on October 22, 2019, motherjones.com/politics/2012/06/gops-dead-end-marriage-program/.

order, which contributes to this renewed positioning of marriage as aspirational."[59] From a consumer capitalist perspective, if women are delaying marriage or choosing not to marry at all, the marriage narrative had to be reintegrated into ideals of individual achievement and choice to reinvigorate the wedding industry's profits.

As the significance of marriage for economic security or the purpose of raising children diminished for women, a cultural economy and mythos has re-emerged around it. Cultural theorist Angela McRobbie wrote, "... the paraphernalia of marriage culture assumes much visibility within popular culture at the very moment when its necessity is being put into question."[60] This also became the case as marriage equality became a major focus (and point of internal contention) within the LGBTQ movement and "same-sex" marriage became legal state by state, and then federally. It was not just the right to love and build a family on equal footing that was increasingly available to a wider part of the population, but the expectation and opportunity to participate in and subscribe to marriage culture and contribute to the wedding industry. The slew of weddings I attended in my early thirties certainly reflected and illustrated this societal shift. Similar to neoliberal, "choice" feminism, the couples who organized them considered every detail of their wedding to reflect their individual taste and preferences, as opposed to reflecting a larger political dynamic.

---

59 Jia Tolentino, "'Marriage Changes When You Don't Just Need A Warm Body and a Paycheck': A Talk With Rebecca Traister," Jezebel, published March 3, 2016. jezebel.com/marriage-changes-when-you-dont-just-need-a-warm-body-an-1762007106

60 Angela McRobbie, *The Aftermath of Feminism: Gender, Cultural, and Social Change* (London: Sage, 2009), 62.

Marriage has not only been positioned as an economic and professional capstone for middle, upper, and creative class professionals, but as a means to self-actualization. More women are now able to be financially stable without marriage, a departure from the mid-twentieth century. Yet, wedding blogs, Instagram, and women's magazines are full of stories about how marriage enables someone's "best self" to emerge and to reach for previously impossible sounding dreams. In her introduction to *Wife, Inc.* Suzanne Leonard writes about how this embrace of marriage in popular and mainstream feminist culture is very different from critiques radical feminists levied against the institution of marriage during the 1960s and 70s. She explains, "The idea that marriage was not a shackle but instead a worthwhile and even emancipatory commitment represented a significant shift from the 1970s, when marriage's restrictive strictures invited significant backlash."[61] The contemporary, neoliberal feminist approach towards marriage is to loosen those strictures instead undoing them all together.

This emphasis on personal fulfillment and the idea that marriage is an exercise of free choice, Leonard explains, perfectly fits a neoliberal ideology and the rhetoric of "choice feminism." Making marriage a vehicle for self-fulfillment also serves to imbue it with a kind of mystical, transformative power while obscuring the fact that it largely supports a system that is based on heterosexism, gender, class, and racial inequality. As marriage is increasingly only available to those with the economic means to do so, and people tend to marry within their racial and

---

61 Suzanne Leonard, *Wife Inc.: The Business of Marriage in the Twenty-First Century* (New York: New York University Press, 2018), 10.

ethnic groups, it is also a source of class and racial stratification. However, many people who had identified with punk and Riot Grrrl's radical critique of how patriarchy and dominant culture influenced their intimate lives made choices to marry.

In my early thirties, I was under the thrall of marriage as a fix for disappointments in my own life. After I broke off a serious relationship, I viewed the relationship's failure as my own, not the fact that I was dating an alcoholic I did not love. I had taken the rhetoric of marriage as women's personal choice and sign of achievement into dangerous territory: I believed that I had not achieved personal fulfillment through this particular relationship because there was something wrong with me and I didn't work hard enough. Riot Grrrl's insistence that we create revolution in the intimate spaces of our lives, when internalized and understood without a broader agitation for social change, can threaten to cross the line into choice feminism. If we are responsible for bringing a "do it yourself" philosophy into your life and feminism, it can be too easy to blame yourself when you feel like you haven't measured up to a feminist ideal. However, a key dimension of intersectional feminism is the fact that feminism is not just about our personal actions, but how those contribute to and connect with movements for collective liberation and work to undo intersecting structures of oppressive power.

Weddings simplify complexity, temporarily banish the boredom of couplehood, and create a romantic narrative out of a relationship's day-to-day struggles. While modern marriages are positioned as valuing equity, shared responsibility, and mutual respect and are seen as a space of personal freedom and fulfillment, they are often anything but. Statistically women in heterosexual partnerships still do the majority of the housework, about two hours and fifteen minutes a day for women compared to one hour and fifteen minutes a day for men according to the Bureau of Labor Statistics.[62] This didn't take into account the emotional labor women put into relationships: organizing, delegating, scheduling, keeping the feelings of others in mind. This kind of emotional labor by women and femmes enables men to continue to shirk responsibility for ending sexism and prevents actual equity in relationships and society.

Rebecca Traister sums up the challenge for single women, whether they aspire to marriage and raising children or not, of existing in a political and social world that was not created to center them. She writes, "If we are to flourish ... we must adjust our economic and social systems, the ones that are built around the presumption that no woman really counts unless she is married."[63] In envisioning the future of marriage, or beyond marriage, we must also envision and work for a more equitable society not based on the unit of the couple.

Punk feminist values posit that we are responsible for building community and bringing meaning to our lives, not waiting for validation from within established systems. Finding other avenues of meaning and identity outside of being part of a couple is essential for the well-being of everyone, whether they are in a relationship or not. For many women this means confronting the fear of becoming a cliche and resisting all the cultural baggage

62 bls.gov/tus/charts/household.htm
63 Traister, 299.

that is piled upon single women: that she is bitter, unlovable, too ambitious, ugly, frigid, too demanding, and all together culturally unworthy. Riot Grrrl, and punk attitude, shows the way for this, sneering "so what if I am" back at these fears, embracing being singular and difficult as an act of resistance.

In her book *Spinster* Kate Bolick points out that the choice to be married or single is actually a false binary—the important question for her is whether women are considered full people capable of determining their own lives.[64] Briallen Hopper expands upon the power of the spinster and the rejection of traditional heterosexual coupling, writing. "Historically, spinsterhood has meant a kind of radical unavailability to straight men ... This sought or unsought rejection has the potential to be experienced by women as a source of strength. It can mean making the choice not just to set your own terms on the marriage or meat market, but to opt out of the market altogether."[65] Finding strength, community, and intimate friendships with other women and questioning the whole system (or market) in which women are expected to participate also is part of the core tenants of the Riot Grrrl movement.

In a critique of marriage, and homophobia in the cultural and familial structure, Sarah Schulman pushes us to consider a politics beyond marriage equality. She writes, "Relationships keep the social order, but what about when the social order sucks?"[66] Schulman acknowledges that marriage is necessary as a structure for the LGBTQ community to have equal opprtunity

64 Kate Bolick, *Spinster*, New York: Crown Publishers, 2015, 293.
65 Briallen Hopper, *Hard to Love*, New York: Bloomsbury Publishing, 2019, 45.
66 Sarah Schulman, *Ties That Bind*, New York: The New Press, 2009, 130.

to access as heterosexual people because it's a basic, societal acknowledgement that LGBTQ people exist, but pushes her readers to imagine greater. "What I really want is for the shunning [of LGBTQ people] to end," she writes, "I want my books to be equal to your books. I want my death to be equal to your death. I want my feelings to be equal to your feelings and my place in the family to be equal to yours. And when you're mad about something, I want it to be for real reasons that can be articulated, and then I want us to sit down and solve them together. And if I had these things, I would not need gay marriage."[67] What Schulman is underscoring is that if all of us who currently occupy marginalized positions in society had true equality in law and culture, marriage would not be a structure we would need to rely on to organize society. A radical feminist approach to the structure of our lives also means asking a crucial question that goes beyond whether marriage should become antiquated or not. The underlying question that feminists can organize around is how can we work for a society where people of all genders and from all backgrounds are able to inhabit their lives and actualize their dreams in a way that isn't limited by their gender, race, class, sexual orientation, or status as part of a couple?

The kind of choices available to women with advanced degrees and higher paying jobs are often out of reach for poor, working class women who are often immigrants and people of color. Those women are also often shouldering a large burden of unpaid caregiving, whether that's raising children or taking care of the elderly. More equitable social policies that do not revolve

67 Schulman, 131.

around couplehood, or even the structure of the family, could enable the panoply of choices middle and upper class women often have available around marriage, career, education, and starting a family to be available for a wider range of women.

Policies that support white, monied men's self-actualization have been law of the land since this country was founded. Self-actualization should not be limited to the privileged few or something that's pursued purely for personal gain. To be feminists and resist the hegemony of marriage and sexism we must pursue policies that enable the liberation of all. We must also pursue radical solidarity with each other. As Brittney Cooper pointed out, "Patriarchy causes women to succumb to the dog-eat-dog or sister-eat-sister mentality of the relational marketplace, making risky decisions in the name of securing a life partner, while simultaneously reinforcing a market logic in which men can treat women as if they are a dime a dozen...."[68] What does the future of women, gender, and relationships look like if we no longer organize our ambitions, and our social policies, around the couple and the institution of marriage?

Looking deeply at what we really want or need from marriage can reveal deep feelings around loneliness, love, and cultural expectations and biases we don't always see that we carry. Imagining a world beyond legal matrimony can invite us to think creatively, and expansively, about the future. Moving beyond marriage takes the focus off whether or how we will find lasting love or a stable partnership. Rather, it invites us to imagine

68 Brittney Cooper, "All the Single Ladies: Thoughts on the Black Marriage Dilemma," HuffPost, March 18, 2010, huffpost.com/entry/all-the-single-ladies-tho_b_420262, accessed on March 17, 2020.

what kind of world we would live in when the tools we need for a stable, self-actualized life, education, health care, affordable housing, financial stability, and care for the young and the old, are available no matter our gender, race, class, sexuality, or marital, employment, or immigration status.

Marriage hardly seems like a benign, individual choice or a pathway to personal emancipation as the conservative movement is again gaining strength, stacking the judiciary, and attacking the basic rights and freedoms of women, people of color, immigrants, and the LGBTQ community. Our future *depends* upon rethinking marriage and couplehood. Can we imagine a world where we could shed all the narratives and outsized and outdated hopes we've placed in the single institution of marriage? What space would it open up emotionally and politically? What would the 76-billion dollar wedding industry stand to lose, and how would it fight against a move away from marriage? How does questioning marriage question capitalism?

Briallen Hopper echoes these questions, writing, "There are urgent reasons why spinsters need to look beyond the self and resist the system … Marriage is still an important legal and social category with implications for many practical and symbolic aspects of adult life. Because in our culture, marriage is a choice, but it also isn't. It's a rom-com ending and a party with a cake, but it's also a systemic mechanism that separates the enfranchised from the disenfranchised, the included from the excluded."[69] In addition, as Hopper also acknowledges, us spinsters are indebted to communities that have been barred from marriage by law or

---

69 Hopper, 52.

demographics, or for whom marriage fails to protect, such as those torn apart by family separation at the border or incarceration, who have long needed to come up with "alternative" structures of care. Brittney Cooper also addresses this in an essay about the challenges professional Black women have long faced when it comes to partnership and marriage, "First, perhaps we need to rethink our investments in the traditional nuclear family, since we have historically never really had the mom, dad, 2.5 kids and a dog model in African American communities anyway. That's the fault of slavery, not Black pathology ... The reality is that for many of us to find the love we want, a blended family will be in our future."[70] Finding alternatives to "traditional" marriage isn't so much of a new or radical idea, but rather, recognizing, celebrating, and centering what many communities are already practicing.

Moving beyond marriage looks like healthy relationships, friendly, familial, and romantic; diverse communities; and supportive, inclusive social policies. If we put even half as much energy into working for this dream as we do planning and spending on our dream weddings, our future could look very different and very bright. And I can toast to that.

---

70 Brittney Cooper, "All the Single Ladies: Thoughts on the Black Marriage Dilemma," HuffPost, March 18, 2010, huffpost.com/entry/all-the-single-ladies-tho_b_420262, accessed on March 17, 2020.

BEYOND A SEAT AT THE TABLE

"And She Gathered All before Her
And She made for them A Sign to See
And lo They saw a Vision
From this day forth Like to like in All things
And then all that divided them merged
And then Everywhere was Eden Once again"

- Entryway banners for Judy Chicago's *The Dinner Party*

This is what visitors see upon entering *The Dinner Party,* Judy Chicago's iconic, room-sized feminist art oeuvre: A massive triangular table glistening with ornate ceramic plates and chalices that seemed to hover above their embroidered table runners. The first place setting is the Primordial Goddess, and features a china plate with a deep red streak running through its center. The next plate, for Kali, has an opening that reveals further folds, like eggs or teeth. Next to her the Amazon's plate is flanked with glinting silver axes and gilded nipples, for their armor. Moving further around the table, Emily Dickinson is frozen in pink, frilly lace, and Margaret Sanger's plate glowers a throbbing, bright red, with bulbous, ceramic curves. Names of women spill in gilded calligraphy across the pearly ceramic floor: Nefertiti, Mary Magdalene, Juana de la Cruz, Radclyffe Hall… and then in clear script, just near one of the triangles' points: Copyright Judy Chicago 1979.

The Elizabeth A. Sackler Center for Feminist Art opened at the Brooklyn Museum in 2007 with *The Dinner Party* as its cornerstone piece. But the road to a permanent home had not been easy. Judy Chicago debuted the piece in 1979, first at the SFMoMA and then at the Brooklyn Museum, but after other tour dates were cancelled due to cultural backlash from the art world she struggled to find institutions to present it. Women's groups raised money to bring it to community spaces, believing they were bringing a piece of women's history to their city. It was almost acquired in the 1990s for the University of the District of Columbia, but they backed down amid fears that it was "controversial," especially after pro-life Congressman Robert K. Dornan, declared it ceramic, 3D pornography.[71] It was a prime example of the "culture wars" of the early 1990s, where politicians, academics, funding institutions, and members of the media debated whose "values" would come to represent or define American culture. Those who traditionally held cultural power, Protestant white men, were being pushed to broaden access to that power, and abortion, sexuality, LGBTQ issues, and race, racism, and culture, and where funding went, were all being debated.

When I first viewed *The Dinner Party* with my friend Lauren in the early 2000s we wrote it off as a product of essentialist, second wave feminism. As many other feminists have pointed out, the fact that the majority of the women featured at the table were white, and most of the non-Western women at the table were part of the ancient world or mythical goddesses reinforced an idea that women of color were better if they were exotic, ancient, or imaginary in the eyes of white feminists. For many feminists who considered themselves part of, or post, "third wave" feminism, the ideas that inspired second wave feminists during the 1960s and 70s were already dusty museum pieces, even though sexism

71*The Dinner Party*, Wikipedia, accessed on April 25,2020. en.wikipedia.org/wiki/The_Dinner_Party#Controversy_at_the_University_of_the_District_of_Columbia

in the art world, and the world at large, was not. Third wave feminists centered an understanding of the intersectionality of identities and movements. They critiqued the power held by white feminists and moved away from the idea that all women essentially shared similar experiences because of their anatomy (or that it was necessary to share anatomy to be a woman) and towards a postmodern understanding of gender and womanhood as a construct.

However, the piece remained controversial not only for the ceramic vulvas, essentialist idea of women, or the exclusion of women of color. The construction of the piece had relied on the volunteer labor of over 400 artists and community members. They researched the women who were honored at the table, wove the tapestries for the entry banners, and embroidered the intricate table runners. They helped sculpt, paint, and fire the oversize china plates and built the frame for the table. Their work drew comparisons to a renaissance atelier with Chicago acknowledging, "The studio gradually became a structure of self-sufficient groups working under my guidance while also building teamwork through shared responsibility and honest dialogue."[72] And yet it was Judy Chicago's name and copyright that was on the piece, causing resentment among the hundreds of artists who had collaborated with her.

I began working at the Brooklyn Museum as an educator and public programmer before the opening of the center, giving me a front row seat to the debates about *The Dinner Party*,

72 Acknowledgement Panels, The Brooklyn Museum. Accessed on April 25, 2020. brooklynmuseum.org/eascfa/dinner_party/acknowledgement_panels

and Chicago's vision for it, that still raged. During a public conversation between Chicago and Elizabeth Sackler, the Feminist Art Center's benefactor, the issue came to a head. A long-time friend of Chicago's, Sackler was the heir to a medical advertising fortune, a well-known philanthropist, and a board member at the Brooklyn Museum. Chicago perched her diminutive frame in an armchair on the large stage, her orange-red hair fanning out like a fiery mane, wearing dark glasses and brown lipstick. During the question and answer period a woman with a greying ponytail sitting in the front row stood up and demanded answers.

"Where are the acknowledgement panels? In every other exhibition the names of the people who worked on *The Dinner Party* have been displayed with it and now our work, our labor, has been erased. This was a community effort, and the artists have been demanding greater recognition for years!"

Judy Chicago zeroed in on her like a hawk.

"Listen," she began, her voice pitched and commanding, "This piece is my vision. Everything that went on *The Dinner Party* I directed or designed. It's mine."

"Women have been erased from history once again!" declared the woman. "Shame on you and shame on the Brooklyn Museum!"

When Lauren and I first saw the piece, like many feminists of our generation, we thought that the artists, activists, and ideals of second wave feminism were museum pieces themselves, confined to history. But many of the people who shaped the movement were still very much alive and active. I realized I had a stereotypical image of second wave feminists in my head as dowdy, out of it, and passe, no doubt shaped by the media backlash to feminism I was exposed to growing up in the 1980s. How had a monumental piece like *The Dinner Party* frozen them and our contemporary ideas about the feminist movement during the seventies in time and and reduced it to a few simple talking points: essentialist, kitschy, exclusionary of women of color? And as third wave feminists, in our zeal to tell our own stories and fashion feminism in our image, as well as to avoid shaming and lecturing from second wave feminists, what had we shoved aside?

In 2007 feminist art was on the tip of the New York City museum world's tongue. Articles in newspapers, magazines, and art journals all asked whether feminism's new centrality to the contemporary art world was here to stay, despite the fact feminist art and artists had been working, showing, and protesting consistently since the 60s. But the history of the feminist art movement was much like the history of Riot Grrrl. Often written off by, and shut out of, the mainstream art world, women artists formed their own communities to nurture, sustain, show, and support each other's art. They were often hosted in ephemeral spaces or squeezed in between other responsibilities. In the 1970s and 80s women founded collectively run galleries like A.I.R. and SOHO 20. Groups like the Guerilla Girls and the Ad Hoc Women's Art Committee protested the lack of representation of women artists, and especially women of color, at New York's Metropolitan Museum of Art and the Whitney Biennial, respectively. Judy Chicago herself, frustrated with the male dominated and overly formalist LA art scene of the late 60s and 70s, began a women's art program in Fresno and later moved it to CalArts. In an interview with Lucy Lippard she told her, "The only thing I could do was commit myself to developing an alternate community based on the goals and ideas of women…"[73] These community-driven projects and initiatives were largely treated as un-serious or not "real" art by the majority of the art world, but they created dialogue and touch points about the narrow treatment of artists who were women, people of color, and part of the LGBTQ community. While some individual artists, such as Barbara Krueger and Cindy Sherman, did find commercial success, especially as the art world embraced postmodernism in the 80s and 90s, in general feminist art as a movement had been shut out of mainstream institutions.

Riot Grrrl, and punk more broadly, also had found its home in improvised and borrowed spaces. When Riot Grrrls demanded that punk respect girls and take feminism seriously, similar to the feminist artists of the 60s and 70s, they were often dismissed by mainstream critics and culture. The music made by Riot Grrrls was written off as "girl bands" as opposed to being part of a more serious canon of punk or rock music. In the late 1990s *Spin* magazine published a list of the top 200 rock bands of all time and a paltry few were made by women—missing were generation defining albums like Bikini Kill's *Pussy Whipped* or Sleater-Kinney's *Dig Me Out*. According to the chroniclers of mainstream rock it was as if the Riot Grrrl and the subsequent popularity of "girl bands" had never happened. Similar to the art world, the impact of feminist rock music wasn't considered part of the overall story of the culture until much later.

73 Lucy Lippard, "Judy Chicago, Talking to Lucy Lippard" in *From The Center: Feminist Essays on Women's Art*, New York: E.P. Dutton & Co, 1976, 218.

As Riot Grrrl-inspired feminists grew up, they sang along to Le Tigre's 1999 song *Hot Topic,* which paid homage to feminist artists past and present. The song tried to encourage maturing Riot Grrrls to look into feminist art history. However, there were still a limited number of galleries, journals, and outlets available to show work and find the work of other artists besides those we created ourselves. These were marginal, borrowed, and ephemeral spaces that were a far cry from prime museum real estate. The idea that we could access mainstream art spaces felt as remote as the second wave feminism that we often critiqued.

When the Brooklyn Museum announced the opening of the Center for Feminist Art, artists flooded the institution with emails, letters, and phone calls, desperate for inclusion and recognition. While a feminist approach to art making and the business of art could emphasize collaboration and mutual support, the center seemed to function more as business as usual for the art world: artsits and curators trying to further their careers, while the institution worked to court and please donors. The center was the first of its kind, and feminist artists, critics, and art historians felt that if they were not included they would be written out of history, a fear that Judy Chicago's approach to the artists she had worked with on *The Dinner Party* threatened to confirm. As the art world and press reconsidered feminist art, a competitive friction crackled between institutions, artists, and curators: who could host a symposium with the most attendance and coveted tickets? Who would net that big grant? Who would get reviewed by *The New York Times*?

The competition and careerism in the feminist art world was a reflection of a tension that has long existed between more "liberal" and "radical" feminism: does feminist art and activism aim to make the current system and powerful instutitions more broad and inclusive, or does it aim to dismantle them entirely? Can feminists, and feminist art, do both? What role does funding and money play, especially when donors are also pushing their own agenda? What happens when former radicals are brought inside and supported by those institutions they pushed against? Do they protect what they perceive as theirs or keep fighting for a more expansive, just world?

The moment in 2007 when the feminist art center opened was an unsure, scary time for many parts of the feminist movement. It was a movement under constant attack after Bush's two presidential terms. At that time, cultural feminism was also fighting back from being regarded as a footnote of the 1970s and 1990s activist and subcultural movements. Feminist art, besides for a few big superstars, survived in intimate settings of artist collectives, community galleries, and journals operating in semi-obscure corners of academia. The Center for Feminist Art represented a beacon of collective hope that feminist voices would finally be heard and taken seriously inside a respected cultural institution.

The center was also a source of skepticism and fear in the feminist art community. The artists who had created and protected these spaces, often at great personal cost, felt alarmed when there was suddenly an institution with the authority and funding to construct a history of feminist art. They realized they may not be included and were fearful that, after being attacked on all sides, they would be written out of the very movement they had nurtured. And even as the museum tread carefully, and acknowledged telling only one part of the story of feminist art, by virtue of the prestige afforded by that platform the curated version of the story carried an important cultural weight. The cultural change that can be created by feminist art can take years to ripple through mainstream culture and it is difficult, if not impossible, to contain its power and messiness within the walls of an institution. Much of the power of contemporary feminist art comes from its multiplicity—the fact that contemporary feminism isn't one narrative, but many, and that there is still much power to be critiqued and undone.

In bringing feminism into the institution and giving feminist artists a platform, the Center for Feminist Art also laid bare the power dynamics that fracture a feminist approach to coalition and culture building. Instead of really listening to each other, we were each struggling to stake our individual claim and use the logic of feminism to build our own power and accomplish our own goals. The Center for Feminist Art, for all its revolutionary rhetoric, was still mired in capitalist careerism and neoliberal ideals.

Over a decade later, feminism is no longer pronounced a "dead" part of the art world, but rather is now a label to sell cool art. A t-shirt reading "You are nothing without feminist art" designed by Sarah Faith Gottesdiener became a cult best seller. Judy Chicago had a cover shoot for the *T, The New York Times'* glossy fashion and lifestyle magazine. Elizabeth Sackler has handed out awards at a high-priced museum luncheon to everyone from the Guerilla Girls and Angela Davis to Miss Piggy to recognize their pioneering feminist spirits, and fabulously feted the center's tenth anniversary in 2017. The successful feminists celebrated by the likes of the cultural elite, like Elizabeth Sackler, are media-savvy and possess the ever important skill of polishing themselves as a recognizable brand. By design, both museums and popular culture exactingly smooth out and lump together disparate ideas, movements, and artists in the name of scholarship, making a statement, or selling a product.

The idea that art can be feminist has entered mainstream culture in an unanticipated way. In 2007 it seemed unimaginable that feminist memoirs like those by Roxane Gay or Rebecca Solnit's essay collection *Men Explain Things to Me* could be best sellers; that a pop star like Beyonce could sample Chimamanda Ngozi Adichie's "We should all be feminists" and pay homage to the videos of Pipilotti Rist on her *Lemonade* visual album; that the corporate feminism popularized by Sheryl Sandberg's *Lean In* could become a regular household conversation; the storm of change inspired by the #MeToo movement; and that Bikini Kill had not only reunited but sold out huge venues all around the world.

Mainstream cultural embrace of feminism has opened needed, widespread conversations around sexual violence, the gender and racial wage gap, body image, and the treatment of women of color and immigrant families, but overall this attention has not translated into concrete policy. Political misogynist movements are rapidly gaining strength, helped tremendously by the Presidency of Donald Trump. Issues that have been core to feminist organizing for decades, like reproductive rights, benefits for single parents and working families, education, safety from violence, and equal treatment in the workplace have been rapidly eroded, especially for immigrant women and women of color. Tensions around whether feminism should focus on broadening the system to make it more accessible to all or tearing it down all together, and the role of money and power within this, are still high. However, grassroots movements led by feminists are also springing up and growing, whether they are internationally reaching, like Black Lives Matter, or hyper local, such as organizing neighborhood mutual aid networks and information sharing for immigrant rights.

The revolutionary, scrappy, on-the-ground spirit of radical feminist art can still buoy our movements for justice. Instead of pushing to be part of a curated institution or sponsored by a major brand, feminist artists and activists must look to the future. Feminist art continues to live in those intimate, community-minded spaces that incubated radical feminist thought for so long, and it is fighting back against attacks on our communities and building grassroots mutual aid networks. Cultural change is slow and the behind the scenes work in all movements is thankless. That's why we need visionary art, cultural memory, and on-the-ground organizing to carry us through difficult times, to learn from past struggles and appreciate how artists carved out time to create during them. Feminist art doesn't romanticize those struggles, but pushes its viewers to keep our vision clear. Liberatory feminist art can keep making a wider, more complex cultural vision possible, even as the ideals and images of feminism are approrpriated by mainstream culture and institutions.

Feminist artists are informed by different histories and experiences, and create their art to disrupt the status quo and to speak out. They have different reasons and ways for identifying as "feminists." They are not a streamlined package, on message and in agreement. Riot Grrrl and feminist artists in the 90s and 2000s pushed to elevate "craft" to the status of fine art, and use discarded materials, our bodies, and performance as art, while starting our own art galleries, journals, and art and activists collectives—all of which feminist artists had done long before us. Us snotty punks, of course, thought we invented these tactics, but we were really continuing a conversation started by artists generations earlier.

Like contemporary feminism, second wave feminism was anything but monolithic, all-white, straight, humorless, or only attuned to the needs of middle class women: Faith Ringgold demonstrated that quilting was a form of fine art; Adrian Piper helped define and illustrate the idea of gender and race as performance; Lynda Benglis skewered the male art world with her full page ad in Art Forum showing her naked, greased, tan body brandishing an oversized dildo; organizations like Black Women Artists and the Lesbian Art Project organized group shows and performances and pushed for art by women of color and queer artists to be taken seriously; collectives like the Women's Action Coalition and, of course, the Guerrilla Girls used costumes and humorous rallying calls to draw attention to the lack of representation of women in major galleries and museums and the economic disparities between men and women artists.

Feminist art is essential to reimaginging our world because it is bold, complicated, messy, grandiose, and intimate. Effective feminist art doesn't just insist those of us left out of institutional power get a seat at the table of history, culture, and politics or a feminist donor's luncheon celebrating women's accomplishments, but knocks down those tables and provides a bluprint for building a more inclusive, just, and expansive table. It makes us rethink our assumptions and look at the world differently. It bothers us and sticks with us and motivates us to action.

PART THREE

FIGHTING INJUSTICE AND BUILDING FEMINIST POWER

OUR BODIES ARE NOT OURSELVES

"Why do you think that advertisements that depict unrealistic visions of women are harmful?" asked our high school biology teacher. Our freshman class had just dutifully watched *Killing Us Softly*, Jean Kilbourne's series on how the media and advertising misrepresent women, reducing them to objects in order to sell products. "Why do those lead us to have unhealthy ideas of how women and girls should look and behave?"

It was the mid-1990s, popular culture was under the sway of teenaged Kate Moss slinging a fashion dubbed, with a sinister overtone, "heroin chic." Waif-like girls swam in grunge-inspired baggy jeans and oversized Calvin Klein tank tops, or flounced about in pastel baby doll dresses, their feet weighed down with heavy Doc Martens. Meanwhile, mothers fretted over facts about young women's plummeting self-esteem. Nervously they discussed pressures put on women, especially white women, to conform to unrealistic beauty standards that led to eating disorders and the desire for cosmetic surgery. Many parents learned from Naomi Wolf's *The Beauty Myth*, first published in 1990, Dr. Mary Pipher's 1994 book *Reviving Ophelia: Saving the Selves of Adolescent Girls*, or a myriad of melodramatic movies depicting white, popular girls suffering from eating disorders and perpetuating the myth that disordered eating was a white women's issue.[74]

---

74 Michelle Konstantinovsky, "Eating Disorders Do Not Discriminate" Slate, March 20, 2014, available at: slate.com/human-interest/2014/03/eating-disorders-and-women-of-color-anorexia-and-bulimia-are-not-just-white-girl-diseases.html.

When my mother had tried to talk to me about the dangers of extreme dieting and the threat of anorexia, I rolled my eyes in dismissive, teenage disdain. Sure, I had friends on my field hockey team who had only Diet Coke for lunch and incessantly chewed gum to fight their hunger pangs, but I didn't yet feel that their obsession over their weight and appearance applied to me. It was soon after we watched *Killing Us Softly* that I discovered the zines *It's a Big Fat Revolution* and *I'm So Fucking Beautiful* penned by musician, writer, and fat activist Nomy Lamm.

"Remember: Fat Oppression is a form of institutionalized oppression," Nomy scrawled in the second issue of *I'm So Fucking Beautiful*.[75]

She went on to write a list of rules for non-fat people to keep in mind about those considered "fat" including, "Fat people do not lack control," and "Diets are 29 times more unhealthy than being fat." At the end of the list, in a slightly larger font, "If you consider me a threat, if you fear me now, just wait. The fat grrrl revolution has begun! Fat Grrrl = Punk Fuckin' Rebel!"

Her urgent scrawl blew Jean Kilbourne's rational, second-wave feminist analysis out of the water. In *It's a Big Fat Revolution* Nomy viscerally summarized and rebuked mainstream attitudes about fat people, especially women.

"All my life the media and everyone around me have told me that fat is ugly. Which of course is just a cultural standard that has many, many medical lies to fall back upon," she wrote. "I am not dieting anymore because I know that this is how my body is

75 Lamm, Nomy. n.d. *I'm so fucking beautiful*. Olympia, WA: Nomy Lamm.

supposed to be, and this is how I want it to be. Being fat does not make me less healthy or less active. Being fat does not make me less attractive... I know that the unhappiness is not a result of my fat. It's a result of a society that tells me I'm bad."

Nomy didn't just want accountability in advertising and the media, or to politely analyze how it ripped women's bodies apart. She wanted revolution.

"Where's the revolution?" she asked, "My body is fucking beautiful, and every time I look in the mirror and acknowledge that, I am contributing to the revolution."

Revolutionary. Punk fuckin' rebel grrrl. Through Nomy's zine many Riot Grrrls, myself included, were able to discover a whole network of zines written by and for other fat women and gender nonconforming people, volumes of underground writing that became a growing movement that not only promoted fat positivity, but fat liberation. Nomy Lamm and her friends weren't fretting that the sexist, impossible beauty standards churned out by the advertising industry were killing them softly. They weren't worrying over their lost selves. They were loudly declaring themselves and rebelling against the way advertising, fashion, and mainstream media tried to make larger people, especially women, feel inadequate, insecure, and invisible.

While "Riots Not Diets" was a key slogan throughout Riot Grrrl, and many grrrls discussed their relationship to their bodies, Riot Grrrl zines that specifically interrogated fatphobia and discrimination against fat people also brought an intersectional approach, and revolutionary energy, to their thinking about body image. Zinester Kristy Chan confronted racist beauty standards that validate thin, white women, writing in *Evolution of a Race Riot,* "I don't deserve to feel that I am ugly when I should be pissed. I also started to think about how issues of race affect me from reading different zines and such where most of the time, race is discussed from a white privileged viewpoint."[76] In thinking about the idea of whiteness as the "perfect" body for women, Riot Grrrls connected resistance to beauty standards and white supremacy.

The radical feminist, fat positive movement's message of loving yourself for who you were and how you moved through the world was informed by intersectional, queer feminist politics. Altogether it was an approach that exploded what had been considered "socially acceptable" around bodies and gender and embraced radical ideas about celebrating, not shaming, our unique bodies and selves. I was proud to proclaim "Fat solidarity!" and "Riots not diets!" and I vowed to be an ally to fat women everywhere. With determined gusto I declared that traditional beauty standards for women did not, and would never, apply to me.

In the early 2000s Krissy Durden, author of the fat-rights zine *Figure 8,* started a fat girls cheerleading squad. They wore coordinated outfits and jumped and clapped to body positive chants like, "Now I'm feeling healthy and ready to riot / Against those demands that I need to diet! / I will take up space and love my size / Cuz fat and fabulous is on the rise!"

---

76 Kristy Chan in *Evolution of a Race Riot,* Mimi Mguyen, Ed. Berkeley, CA, 1997, 44.

Chanting along with their rallying cries, I felt punk as I pushed away the nasty attitudes of those who judged and discriminated against fat people. The budding "fat positive," or its radical cousin fat liberation, movements were still underground and felt cutting edge and radical. However, as I clapped my hands to celebrate beauty in all shapes and sizes, I realized that no one had ever directly made me feel like my success and worth was tied to how my body looked.

The irony in much of the fat positive attitudes that informed Riot Grrrl was that many participants, like myself at the time, were thin, or had bodies that conformed to "acceptable" sexist beauty standards. While sexism and patriarchy create a constantly moving target for women's bodies and fatphobia impacts everyone no matter what their size—women's bodies are always a target of shame no matter what—there is a power difference between those who experience fat oppression on a day-to-day basis because of their body size and those who do not.

However, Riot Grrrl's style of outright rejection of "fascist beauty standards" (as one slogan read) was harder to sustain as I, and many others who had been influenced by it, began to build our lives outside of the subcultural, radical feminist bubble. In my early 30s, my body began to shift, as everyone's does due to age and metabolism. I had spent a decade doing office work that included mostly sitting and marinating in the constant banter of fussing about and shaming one's body that so often constitutes small talk and bonding among women. Previously, I had never thought of my body as a burden, a privilege I hadn't fully realized I carried. As I advanced into my thirties the social pressure I had kept at bay through my teens and twenties via eye rolls and Riot Grrrl inspired feminism, it had started to wear through my defenses.

I had believed rejecting prevailing attitudes about how women's bodies were supposed to be was a one time action. Like other forms of institutional oppression, I underestimated the impact of the sheer persistence and volume that negative messages about women's bodies could have on me, especially as my body changed. Intellectually, I understood that we exist in a habitus of self-hatred, that our daily behavior, patterns of interaction, and social ideals were based on and reinforced by damaging ideas of ultra-feminine beauty that we internalized, accepted, and perpetuated as normal. Being perceived as "feminine" is part of a rubric of success in the workplace for many women. I felt what the Council on Size and Weight Discrimination has proven to be true: "plus-size" workers are discriminated against. On average they are paid $1.25 less than "average-size" workers, which could add up to as much as $100,000 over their career.[77]

In American culture weight loss is so often touted as "transformation" and tied to so much more than just our bodies. In my early thirties I also craved transformation, admiration, and to be seen as a serious, professional woman who was in control of her own future. Weight loss is often conflated with "empowerment" and "personal responsibility," which are also tenets of neoliberal feminism. I enrolled in Weight Watchers, seeking the feeling of being in control when much of my life was not, and spent the next few years in weekly meetings, perched on

---

77 cswd.org/statistics-2

the edge of a folding chair in a local synagogue among a group of majority women collecting metallic stickers as awards for weight loss milestones, clapping politely as others in the group reached their goals. It was the polar opposite of the raucous clapping and radical rejection of diet culture that had been shared by the fat cheerleaders years before.

Despite my frustration at needing to restrict and control what I ate, dieting became an easy, almost lazy, mechanism through which to bond with other women. Connecting over dissatisfaction or hatred of our bodies was behavior ingrained from an early age. According to reports by The Eating Disorder Foundation and Common Sense Media, the average age women start dieting is eight. Participating in a diet program shifted my attitude around food: Instead of a source of nourishment or pleasure, it became a substance to be controlled. Instead of relieving my anxiety around my weight and my body, being in a weight loss program pushed that anxious energy towards food as a means of physical and emotional control. I looked at exercise purely as a way to "earn" more food, rather than as an activity that was enjoyable or a path to building strength, power, and long term health. Weight Watchers caused a collision between my perfectionist tendencies and my feminism: a deep part of me wanted to prove I could match and beat any standard, no matter how absurd, while I was also angry at how those beauty standards damage all of us, of all genders and gender presentations. While I told myself losing weight was about my health and I was making a conscious, feminist "choice" to do so, my attitude mirrored long held, dangerous beliefs about women's bodies.

As I lost weight, strangers and family members alike complimented me on my "transformation," reinforcing the idea of my body as a currency that was directly tied to my self-worth. I had craved transformation along with weight loss, and I convinced myself to stick with it by buying into the promise that it was part of a larger effort to single-handedly reshape my life. It would be several years before Sheryl Sandberg's book *Lean In* came out, but I adopted the same flawed, neoliberal, take ownership of your life and "lift yourself up by your bootstraps" attitude which it utilizes as its thesis. I lost a sense of a bigger picture and the connection between structural inequality and my own life. Instead, I viewed the work before me through the lens of personal choice and individual empowerment and did not recognize that I had turned to controlling my body instead of proactively addressing the more emotionally complex aspects of my life.

My initial enthusiasm about the restrictions imposed by Weight Watchers and my weight loss success had turned into a feeling of rage about being controlled by them. I felt exhausted and burnt out on tracking every bite, lick, and taste I ate and every step I took. Instead of turning that rage towards larger forces at play in my life or considering how controlling every bit of food intake is not a realistic way to live, I continued to think of food as the vehicle through which to act out my feelings. I stuck myself on the all-too-common cycle of weight gain, dieting, weight loss, frustration, and weight gain. After several half-hearted attempts to restart the punishing daily calculus of recording points, I finally quit Weight Watchers for good.

Nutrition therapists and activists Hilary Kinavey and Dana Sturtevant use the term "backlash eating" and describe it on their blog as a natural, healthy, physiological and emotional response to dieting.[78] They discuss how people, especially women, stuck in the dieting cycle don't take time to learn what their body really needs and what else they need emotionally. Our society is also structured at the core to control and shame women for their bodies, but Kinavey and Sturtevant point out how it's common for women to blame themselves for the resulting weight gain. For many women who consider themselves feminists, this internal struggle and argument is familiar. On her *Dear Sugars* podcast author Cheryl Strayed discusses how, despite her feminism and her iconic status as someone who is living her own truth as a woman, she still has a voice in her head whispering, "Just lose a few more pounds and then you can be happy with your body."[79]

How women are socialized to hate and work to control their bodies also corresponds to how the "ideal" woman in American culture is white and (at least) middle class. Similar to the Riot Grrrls writing over a decade earlier, Virgie Tovar reminds us, "Misogyny works in tandem with white supremacy to build a population of women that is liant and easily manipulated to carry out the oppressive needs of the culture and the state as they currently exist."[80] In addition, much of the criticism and pressure put on women's bodies is shaped through how we are seen as desirable, or not, through the eyes of heterosexual men. Our bodies are a

78 benourished.org/cultivating-body-trust/

79 "Listen to 'Dear Sugars': Trust Your Body — With Hilary Kinavey & Dana Sturtevant," The New York Times, June 9, 2018. nytimes.com/2018/06/09/podcasts/listen-to-dear-sugars-trust-your-body-with-hilary-kinavey-dana-sturtevant.html

80 Virgie Tovar, *You Have the Right to Remain Fat*, New York: Feminist Press, 2018, 72.

currency we redeem for male attention, affection, and validation and this is supposed to be a central focus and driving force in our lives. As Tovar points out, "What we must realize is that it's not thinness that is being eroticisized [by heterosexist patriarchy]. What is being eroticized is the submission thinness represents in our culture… Controlling women's body size is about controlling women's lives."[81] If you are a woman who is both single and fat you are seen as a threat to what women are supposed to conform and aspire to within a white supremacist, heterosexist patriarchy.

What would our lives be like if we could jettison this dialogue and focus on what truly matters to us? And what if what "really matters" is not just self-love, but standing fully in our own power to be better able to contribute to collectively pushing back on, and building alternatives to, the intertwined systems of sexism, capitalism, and racism that work together to control our bodies, minds, and desires? "Ads sell more than products, they sell values, they sell images, they sell concepts of love and sexuality, of success, and perhaps most important, of normalcy. To a great extent they tell us who we are and who we should be," said Jean Kilbourne from a podium to an auditorium of earnest moms and apprehensive teenaged daughters in Killing Us Softly 4.[82] It's not simply resisting advertising and putting forward new or more inclusive beauty standards, it's resisting the culture that creates those ideals altogether, a message Riot Grrrls like Nomy Lamm and Kristy Chan were broadcasting loud and clear. However, living in a white supremacist, heterosexist, capitalist patriarchy, building this resistance requires constant commitment.

---

81 Ibid, 69.
82 Jean Kilbourne, "Killing Us Softly 4: Advertising Images of Women," Media Education Foundation, 2010.

In many ways the revolution that Nomy Lamm and other fat activists of the late 1990s and early 2000s fought for seems to have partially arrived, albeit in a watered down, consumer-capitalism friendly format. Now it's possible to see a slightly wider range of body sizes, as well as ethnic backgrounds and gender presentation, in advertising and mainstream media. Social media platforms are awash in perfectly lighted "plus size fashion influencers" peddling "bo-po" (body positive) content and the latest styles. However, as Lindy West points out, "Buying [body positivity] is one thing, living it is another," and reminds her readers, "Body positivity sells best when it's skinny white models selling it."[83] And certainly, cisgener white women on social media benefit from the "body positivity" movement and the ability to serve as "influencers," while women of color and transgender people face greater trolling, body policing and shaming from other social media users, and often banning or censorship from the platforms themselves.

From activism to academia, the fat liberation movement pushed for a critical understanding of how fatphobia and "weight related belief systems," as Marilyn Wann calls them in her introduction to the *Fat Studies Reader*, inform our cultural attitudes, policies, and activities.[84] That analysis made its way into mainstream culture, but has mostly lost the incitement to revolution and critique of the oppressive systems that created it along the way. Like most radical movements filtered through late capitalism, resistance to oppression has become a bland invitation to celebration and

83 Lindy West, *The Witches are Coming*, New York, Hachette Books, 2019, 213.
84 Marilyn Wann in *The Fat Studies Reader*, Esther Rothblum and Sondra Solovay, eds., New York: New York University Press, 2009, ix.

consumption. Most brands that have adopted a message of body positivity have one goal in mind: to sell us products.

Now advertising instructs women that buying clothes, makeup, skin care products, health food, and skinny girl cocktails is a way to celebrate our self love, practice self care, and focus on our "health." As of 2018, the diet industry was still worth $72 billion in the US alone, and while that value has been falling, a new focus on "health" and "wellness" is making up for it. Reaching towards "health" has become a euphemism for weight loss, dieting, and disordered eating. In the age of celebrity lifestyle brands and designer athleisure wear, health is also being sold as a luxury product and a new rhetoric through which women can channel their body shame and spend their money. "Health has become the stick with which to beat fat people with, and the benchmark for whether body positivity should include someone," wrote Bethany Rutter in an essay in Dazed Digital.[85] For many "plus size" and fat women, the sweaty gym selfie has become a ritual almost to "prove" our effort and commitment to health. Where's the "riots not diets" in that?

Our identities intertwine in many different ways and histories of privilege and oppression impact everyone differently. Capitalism has been successful for so long because its logic is expansive, and as it co-opts and adopts radical movements, it invites us all to keep buying in. Fat women are often expected to present themselves as ultra-feminine, with perfect hair, makeup, and voluptuous curves, using hyper-feminine presentation as a way to protect themselves

---

85 Bethany Ruter, "How 'body positivity' lost its true and radical meaning, Dazed Digital, April 28, 2017, dazeddigital.com/artsandculture/article/35746/1/how-body-positivity-lost-its-true-and-radical-meaning

against age old critiques that fat people are lazy and don't make an effort. While the options are widening, there are still limited socially acceptable ways to be fat, just as there are limited socially acceptable ways to be a woman, queer, or a person of color. And while some brands are expanding their "plus size" offerings, often these clothes are made by women working in sweatshops in the developing world. Is "body positive" fashion truly liberatory if other women are oppressed to create it?

In an article in *Bitch* magazine on the fragility of the body positive movement, writer Evette Dionne reminds us, "as fashion becomes more body positive, the push to make other institutions—including media, law, schools, and housing—more inclusive of people whose bodies have been marginalized has been sidelined... body positivity has morphed to singularly focus on fashion, empowerment, and selling products. It's a complete departure from the radical politics of fat acceptance, the movement that birthed body positivity."[86] Indeed, many of us don't just want space in the mainstream or to be seen as beautiful "despite" our size, we want to create a whole new culture and political system to go along with it that ceases to use our bodies as currency.

Good body, bad body, unruly body, what happens when we radically accept ours no matter what? A true politics of body liberation includes the internal work to let the voices of fear, shame, and self-doubt that are imposed by mainstream culture go. It also asks us to connect fat oppression to other interlinking

---

86 Evette Dionne, '"The Fragility of Body Positivity: How a Radical Movement Lost Its Way," Bitch Magazine, November 21, 2017, bitchmedia.org/article/fragility-body-positivity

systems of oppression. If we are to believe in and practice revolutionary body politics, body liberation should also connect to addressing unequal systems of access to healthy, affordable food, prison abolition, disability justice, and ending sweatshop labor. When considered from an intersectional feminist, anti-captialist perspective, body liberation reaches far beyond the limited confines of consumer friendly "body positivity."

The internal work of fat liberation can start with radical self acceptance. Personally, I had to deeply reconsider and critically examine attitudes that caused me to view my body as a platform for self-improvement that made me worthy of love, attention, health, and success, and framed my "weightloss journey" as a moral pilgrimage. A lifetime of absorbing attitudes from a beauty-obsessed culture, as well as a structured program like Weight Watchers, taught me to equate being thin with my ability to pursue ambitions that had nothing to do with the size of my pants or a number on the scale. "I had been taught to believe that weight loss was the key to all my heart's greatest desires, but the truth is it wasn't. Because you can't find self-love by walking a path saved by self-hatred," writes Virgie Tovar.[87] What if all of us focus on living our lives and organizing against oppressive structures instead of spending countless hours worrying about our weight?

How we feel about our bodies will shift, just as our bodies themselves shift with age and experience. Riot Grrrl-influenced feminism can offer an expansive space for exploring the complexities of that shift. In her zine *Hope* Elissa Nelson wrote

---

87 Virgie Tovar, *You Have the Right to Remain Fat*, New York: Feminist Press, 2018, 110.

about her changing relationship with her body as a queer woman taking dance classes and struggling with illness and injury. She wrote, "A lot of the zines I've read about 'body image' are written by girls who hate their bodies; for me it's always been more complicated than that, especially lately. It's not hate at all, ever; but sometimes it's distrust, and sometimes it's shame, and sometimes it's strength and power. Sometimes it's fear, and sometimes it's a sort of awe."[88] Inspired by similar politics, Meredith Butner launched *When Language Runs Dry*, a compilation zine, and then book, showcasing the experiences of people living with chronic pain and illness. Whether it's expressed and worked out in zines, online publications, podcasts, social media accounts, or any other medium where it's easy to seize the means of production and expression, feminism is a toolbox for learning to embrace how our bodies shift and be curious and investigate where those feelings come from. This approach is the basis of not just radical body acceptance, but also a political practice that is open, expansive, and intersectional.

Adopting a revolutionary attitude towards our bodies is a process and one that is often challenging. While the Riot Grrrl politics summed up in the rallying cry of "Riots Not Diets!" may seem simplistic, Riot Grrrl-inspired body politics are a reminder that our self-hatred, shame, mistrust, and attempts to control our bodies does not serve us. It is also a reminder that while stylish, cute, "plus size" clothes and inclusive advertising campaigns seem like progress, they are not the end goal, and often couched in capitalism, not liberation. Fat liberation and body revolution is

---

88 Elissa Nelson, *Hope*, self-published, 2001.

also about undermining white supremacist, capitalist, patriarchal systems that try to sell us an illusion of our own empowerment.

Confronting attitudes of self-hatred or blame is an invitation to take a deep dive into examining how the intricate web of sexism, heterosexism, racism, and capitalism has shaped our desires and attitudes about ourselves. It is also an invitation to listen to the voices and experiences of others with many different experiences in their bodies and learn from them. In addition, it's an opportunity and responsibility for all of us to take collective action. That may look like resisting policies that aim to blame, punish, and control our bodies, from fighting for greater abortion access to pushing for laws that prevent discriminiation based on weight, to advocating to abolish mass incarceration, protesting police violence against communities of color, fighting for greater rights for people with disabilities, and organizing for more equitable access to healthy food.

One of my favorite shirts is a white tank top that features a curvaceous young woman in a strapless, black dress looking haughty and self assured. It is a reproduction of John Singer Sargent's painting *Madame X and her Ego*, paired with Beyonce's reminder, challenge, and self-affirmation, "I walk like this cause I can back it up," laid over the image in white block letters. I like to pair the top with short shorts and walk down the street, thighs rubbing together, my curves obvious, and dare myself to be thankful for the strength in my body that carries me through this life, and proud of the space that I take up in the world. Or as Kathleen Hanna sang, "In her hips, there's revolution / When she walks, the revolution's coming."

DISCRIMINATION BY DESIGN: BUSINESS, BIAS, THE TROLLS, AND BEING A FEMINIST ON AND OFF THE INTERNET

"The world of coding appreciates your vagina."

My coworkers and I stared at this and other comments piling up under a video of a young teenage girl, a perky blonde YouTube presenter, explaining how she coded her own bracelet, which our company had then 3D printed. The startup where we worked had teamed up with a major tech company on Made with Code, an initiative to get girls into coding. Under the tagline "the things you love are made with code," coding projects like fashion designs, emojis, video games, and 3D printed friendship bracelets were all packaged up in a pastel-hued, rah-rah girl power website.

The comments kept coming and based on their screen names and avatars they all seemed to be from adult men. When we approached our CEO, a white man, about taking the comments down he insisted we leave them open to encourage "dialogue" and "free expression." Instead of deleting the offensive comments, or closing comments on the video all together, one of our community managers was instructed to politely respond to each one. We had just spent significant time and company resources to support a project that encouraged girls to code and we were more concerned with protecting the "free speech" of YouTube trolls than ensuring the intended audience for the project, pre-teen and teenaged girls, felt safe watching it.

The incident I witnessed at work was the mere tip of the tech trolling and discrimination iceberg. However, it is an important reminder that tech companies are companies that have people making conscious decisions behind them and what's at stake for how feminists utilize, build community, and share on the internet.

Like many older millennials who grew up middle class, my first exposure to the internet was in the mid-1990s via AOL chat rooms. Riot Grrrls also found each other through an AOL message board dedicated to them. In the late 1990s and early 2000s feminists connected with other punks, queer people, musicians, and feminists on internet forums and email listservs tailored to their interests, like the Pander Zine Distro and Chainsaw records forums, and Indie Pop List and Typical Girls listserve, which focused on indie pop and women in punk and post-punk music respectively. These forums, popular during "Web 1.0" were often founded and maintained as a labor of love by a person or group of people who were dedicated to building community with like-minded people. With the exception of a few behemoths like AOL, they were often run on open-source or non-profit software and on websites that had been built by hand.

For punk feminists, these online communities felt like the communities that had been forged in person or through the mail via punk shows, buying records from small labels, trading zines, and writing letters, simply extended onto the internet. In many ways, the internet of the 1990s and early 2000s allowed these relationships to strengthen and accelerate due to the ability to communicate in real time without running up a long-distance phone bill. We were approaching the internet with the mindset of punk and zines, and saw it as a medium of community, self-expression, and connection. While these spaces were host to plenty of egos and there were flare ups, trolling, disagreements, and nasty "call outs," they were often moderated and there were clear rules of engagement for the spaces and human moderators who took care to reiterate them.

Backlash against feminist organizing and expression in both online and in-person spaces during the Riot Grrrl-era certainly did occur. Many musicians experienced harassment and threats, which Bikini Kill captured in the intro to their song "White Boy," where a fratty-sounding bro proclaims, "I don't think it's a problem 'cause most of the girls ask for it..." about rape and harassment. Backlash also came in the form of misinterpretation and dismissal by the mainstream media, appropriation of the Riot Grrrl aesthetic, and watering down of its politics by popular culture. It certainly did not rid punk of misogyny, but also the backlash against Riot Grrrl feminism and feminist expression through zines, music, and online platforms did not become a major, unified, violent political force.

The crucial difference between sharing on an internet platform and creating a zine or putting out a record yourself is who owns and controls the means of production and distribution. With something like a zine, for example, you could share it where and with whom you chose. With the rise of web 2.0 or the "social" internet and sites like Facebook and Twitter, as well as smart phones, the potential reach of one's presence became wider and the barrier for entry became lower as technology became more widespread and more widely available. As a result, a greater percentage of the US population also began using the internet, from about 50% of US adults in 2000, to 74% in 2008, to 90% of US adults in 2019.[89] Social media use also grew from 5% of US adults in 2005 to 72% in 2019.[90] As the percentage of people who used the internet rose, so did the potential for profit for companies. The platforms that rolled out with web 2.0 were not designed to facilitate self-expression or democracy. They are not neutral. They were venture-capital backed startup companies whose goal was to exponentially grow their user base in the service of making a profit. Now many of them are publicly traded companies looking to maximize shareholder profits. As a result, in most cases, revenue, especially driven by advertising and data mining, will override keeping platform users safe.

With the majority of the US population online and on social media, who gets amplified, who feels safe, and whose voice is "protected" is a feminist issue. The ability to share one's experience and find community that might not exist or be easy to access in your day-to-day reality is crucial to feeling safe, supported, and coming into yourself as a person. However, with the increase in use and availability of social media also came an increase of internet trolling and online harassment. While internet platforms claim neutrality, it's important to remember, and call out, that these companies are built and run by people making conscious decisions informed by capitalism, sexism, racism, and a host of other biases.

89 Pew Research Center, *Internet/Broadband Factsheet*, accessed on February 19, 2020. pewresearch.org/internet/fact-sheet/internet-broadband/.
90 Pew Research Center, *Social Media Fact Sheet*, accessed on February 19, 2020. pewresearch.org/internet/fact-sheet/social-media/.

Those who take a stand against online harassment and sexism in general often become targets themselves. Game developer, co-founder of independent game company Spacekat, and Congressional candidate Brianna Wu received violent threats for simply being an outspoken woman and leader in the tech and video game sphere. On *This American Life* and in her memoir *Shrill* Lindy West became well-known for confronting and shutting down a troll that impersonated her deceased father. She writes, "There's no 'winning' when it comes to dealing with Internet trolls. Conventional wisdom says, "Don't engage. It's what they want.' Is it? Are you sure our silence isn't what they want? Are you sure that they care what we do at all? From where I'm sitting, if I respond, I'm a sucker for taking the bait. If I don't respond, I'm a punching bag."[91] Outspoken feminist leaders like Lindy West, Brianna Wu, writer and speaker Anita Sarkeesian, actors like Leslie Jones and Kelly Marie Tran, Duchess Meghan Markle, as well as everyday users who are women, gender non-conforming, or from underrepresented groups, have been harassed and driven from online platforms because they have simply had the audacity to think they can express themselves on the internet and have an opinion about comedy, video games, nerd culture, politics, or simply exist as a person online. These cases underline the fact that most major technology companies care more about standing up for anonymous men on their platforms under the rhetoric of "free speech" than they do about encouraging diverse users and robust, inclusive, healthy online communities.

---

91 Lindy West, *Shrill*, New York: Hachette, 2016, 244.

In 2017, a ten-page memo circulated by James Damore, then an engineer at Google, ripped through the internet. By his logic, there are fewer women engineers because women are inherently incapable of the type of thinking required for coding, not because of decades of systemic bias in STEM education and hiring practices. In his screed he proclaimed that "Differences in distributions of traits between men and women may in part explain why we don't have 50% representation of women in tech and leadership."[92] He faulted Google for promoting a culture of "liberal bias" that encouraged more women to work in technical roles. The fact that he had the audacity to feel comfortable circulating such a hateful, rambling public memo throughout an entire global company spoke volumes about how privileged men feel entitled to act at work. For women and underrepresented groups in tech and in the world business in general, the merest slip in "professionalism" can mean losing your job or even the end of your career. Simultaneously, despite very well publicized diversity efforts like Made with Code, Google was also embroiled in a lawsuit alleging pay discrimination and exposing the fact many women were paid far less than men for similar roles. Google fired Damore, but not before he was taken up as a hero in the eyes of white supremacists and "men's rights" activists.

These groups, emboldened after the murder of Heather Heyer as she opposed a white supremacist rally in Charlottesville, Virginia, planned rallies in Mountain View, New York, and Boston, among other cities, to "protest" his firing. Thousands more anti-racist counter protesters turned out and, in most cases, the white

92 Kate Cogner, Exclusive: Here's the Full 10-Page Anti-Diversity Screed Circulating at Google [Updated], Gizmodo, August 5, 2017. gizmodo.com/exclusive-heres-the-full-10-page-anti-diversity-screed-1797564320

supremacists didn't show up at all or quickly retreated. However, like a wildfire jumping a highway, online harassment, intimidation, and discrimination against women and underrepresented groups in tech are not just words on a page site you can ignore. They jump off the screen into tangible actions in the real world.

Nowhere did the connection between online hate speech and hateful actions become more apparent in the mainstream than the storming of the United States Capitol by a group of white supremacists on January 6, 2021 that had been incited and encouraged by then-President Trump's years of violent, racist, and misogynist tweets. Before and throughout his reign as Troll-in-Chief he enabled and encouraged these public showings of white supremacy and sexist violence, though this culture has always been present in American society and in Silicon Valley. Giant blow outs around harassment and discrimination happen so regularly in the tech world we have started to forget about them. They were brought back again to the forefront after the #MeToo movement took hold, and yet the culture did not change.

Companies like Twitter, Google, Facebook, and Reddit are not bastions of democracy and cultivators of community, despite whatever their lofty missions and polished marketing statements may claim. Twitter leadership has admitted, and then readmitted, that they "suck" at protecting users from trolling and abuse. While they temporary banned "alt-right" and white supremacist accounts, it took the Capitol siege for Twitter to permanently ban Trump. While they have used AI and machine learning to eliminate some terrorist groups, such as ISIS, from the platform, Twitter was been reluctant to take a similar approach with white supremacist groups because it could also impact the accounts of prominent Republican politicians.[93] As such, these types of mea culpas fall flat unless a user policy that puts user safety first is not only created, but consistently enforced no matter the power, influence, or wealth of the user. Despite their worldwide influence large tech companies are not the government. They are for-profit companies who can fully allow and decide how their platforms get used and who works for them to build those platforms. They have founders, investors, shareholders, and employees who have a specific stake and are making specific decisions to run these companies and build their wealth and power.

To build less biased, safer, and more accessible tech platforms, tech companies need to recruit, nurture, and promote people from diverse backgrounds, and examine where bias and discrimination may exist in their hiring process as well as overall company culture, policies, and promotion decisions. Tech companies, and companies in general, justify the way they continue to practice discrimination in hiring by using ideas like "excellence" and "culture fit." While they bemoan the lack of a "diverse hiring pool" they don't take the step to work with recruiting firms that specialize in candidates from underrepresented backgrounds, recruit graduates from public or Historically Black Colleges and Universities, or attend and recruit at conferences like Grace Hopper, which regularly draws over 13,000 women working in tech. This all may seem obvious, but it takes effort to step outside the comfort zone of some hiring managers and recruiters and,

93 Joseph Cox and Jason Koebler, "Why Won't Twitter Treat White Supremacy Like ISIS? Because It Would Mean Banning Some Republican Politicians Too." Vice, April 25, 2019. vice.com/en_us/article/a3xgq5/why-wont-twitter-treat-white-supremacy-like-isis-because-it-would-mean-banning-some-republican-politicians-too

unless their job performance is tied to it, they often have little incentive to do so.

How would the industry, the growing companies, and the applications we all use look different if investors insisted that plans for recruiting and retaining diverse candidates, holding unconscious bias training, auditing salaries and promotions for parity, an enforceable employee code of conduct, and a policy to protect users from discrimination and harassment were all in place before they invested in an early-stage startup? As of 2017, in terms of venture capital funded startups, only 8 percent were women, 1 percent were Black, and 0.4 percent were Latina[94]. There are investors and companies like Freada Kapor Klein of Kapor Capital, Ellen Pao of Project Include, and bethanye Blount of Compaas who have already made significant changes in tying more equitable policies to investment, supporting companies who put in the work, and creating systems they can use to ensure greater equity. But they are the industry exception, not the rule.

In the meantime, the onus is on those targeted by trolling to keep ourselves safe and sane online. The work that should have already been done by multi-billion dollar companies falls on the shoulders of their most vulnerable community members. The positive side is that these communities have pushed back, creating robust spaces for resistance, both on- and offline. These spaces often echo, or carry forward, the kind of DIY spirit and taking the pursuit of equity into their own hands that drove movements like Riot Grrrl or earlier feminist collectives like the Combahee

---

94 Transparent Collective, "Underrepresented Founders & VC Funding Raised," available at: transparentcollective.com/who-we-are.html#/, accessed on January 2, 2021.

River Collective. They include organizations that support young women learning to code like Black Girls Code and Girls Who Code, Write Speak Code, a conference to equip diverse women in tech with skills to advocate for themselves and support each other, and Black Twitter, a universe of Black journalists, activists, creatives, and critics, and Hack*Blossom, an organization that helps women, minorities, and gender non-conforming people keep themselves safe online. Tech platforms have also helped amplify the messages and voices of communities of resistance and helped build movements like Black Lives Matter. However, too often "safety" for marginalized community members has involved dropping out of the tech industry or leaving a social media platform, effectively silencing ourselves.

In the end, women and underrepresented groups in tech, and in society in general, don't need more mentoring, networking, and "empowerment" programs. We need actual opportunities, equitable and unbiased hiring and promotion practices, and company cultures that are based on equity and respect. We need spaces where we can connect and share without fear. We demand the same from society more broadly, and we need to continue to forge spaces where we can build strong, resilient communities and movements to drive this kind of change, which may include rethinking capitalism all together. As Jenny Odell writes in *How to do Nothing*, her book pushing against the "attention economy" created by the tech industry, "What if we spent less time shouting into the void and being washed over with shouting in return— and more time talking in rooms to those for whom our words are intended?"[95] A conscious, contextual space, physical or virtual, can also help break the monopoly on community and communication these inequitable platforms are pushing to create.

So much of the punk and Riot Grrrl movements were about creating spaces, whether through zines, shows, or conventions, to connect and build community, which is related to a long history of intentional, anti-authoritarian spaces. While there is an overlap of the punk and open source software movements, it's not just about open source, but thinking about how we structure our communities and live our values on- and offline. What does an expansive, radical space look like in an age further mediated by for-profit tech platforms? How can we use technology to support the forging of intentional spaces that allows us time to strategize, articulate complex points of view, and spend time connecting with each other? This conscious connection, solidarity, and showing up, while it may feel small, can undermine and create viable alternatives to the hyper-capitalist grip tech platforms have on our attention, communities, and lives.

95 Jenny Odell, *How to Nothing: Resisting the Attention Economy,* New York: Melville House, 2019, 176.

PRETTY WHITE WORLDS: RACE AND RECKONING IN RIOT GRRRL AND BEYOND

"**I**t's a privilege, it's a background / It's everything that I own / It's thinking I'm the hero of this pretty white song / It's thinking I'm the hero of this pretty white world," warbled Corin Tucker on Heaven to Betsy's 1994 song *White Girl*.

The song bluntly describes the insidious, and often invisible to white people, attitude around privilege, and captured the attention of many of white women involved in the Riot Grrrl movement who began writing about their white privilege in their zines and singing about it in their bands. In a way this song was indicative of the white Riot Grrrl approach to racism and privilege, which aimed to dissect it while still centering whiteness.

Many versions of Riot Grrrl seemed especially whitewashed. As Mimi Nguyen wrote in her zine *Slant*, published in 1996, "Maybe your oppositional grrrl identity is imagined exclusive of 'Asian' or 'immigrant,' those things that would've made a difference to me, those thing that ensured my involuntary/voluntary exclusion from a much-fabled 'girl unity.'"[96] Racism and white privilege had long been a dividing factor in the Riot Grrrl movement. A notebook Kathleen Hanna wrote in 1991, "How can we make our scenes less white in both numbers + ideology?" went on to note that a program that ecnompasses race, class, and gender relationship must be incorporated from the beginning.[97]

---

96 Mimi Nguyen, "Revolution don't come easy, honey." from *Slant 5*, in *The Riot Grrrl Collection*, Lisa Darms, ed. New York: The Feminist Press, 2013, 306.
97 Kathleen Hanna, "Riot Grrrl Test Patterns," in *The Riot Grrrl Collection*, Lisa Darms, ed. New York: The

Unfortunately, many Riot Grrrls were not as aware of the intersections, or the importance of examining racism and white privilege as Hanna. At a Riot Grrrl Convention in the summer of 1992 in Washington, DC during an unlearning racism workshop co-led by Hanna, some white women claimed "reverse racism" from women of color in the group and were offended and upset they were being asked to consider race, especially when they had just started to feel like they had found a subculture they felt comfortable in.[98] As Ramdasha Bikceem, a Black woman involved in Riot Grrrl and author of the zine *Gunk*, wrote about the convention, "They had a workshop on racism and I heard it wasn't too effective, but really how could it have been if it was filled up with mostly all white girls. One girl I spoke to after the meetings said the Asian girls were blaming all the white girls for racism and that she 'just couldn't handle that.' Ever heard of the word Guilt?? ... Don't get me wrong I am totally for revolution grrrl now... but maybe it shouldn't just be limited to white, middle-class, punk rock grrrls 'cuz there's no denyin' that's what it is."[99] A similar dynamic would play out at other Riot Grrrl conventions throughout the 1990s. It also was one of many discussions about whether the mostly, but not all, white subcultures of punk and Riot Grrrl should try to be more inclusive, or if asking that question in itself continued to center whiteness. These kinds of discussions and debates also showed that while many white Riot Grrrls embraced the idea of intersectionality, they did not embody it or deeply understand that challenging racism and

Feminist Press, 2013, 25.

98 Marcus, 165.

99 Ramdasha Bikceen quotes in Gabby Bess, *Alternatives to Alternatives: the Black Grrrls Riot Ignored*, Vice, August 3, 2015, available at: vice.com/en/article/9k99a7/alternatives-to-alternatives-the-black-grrrls-riot-ignored. Accessed January 31, 2021.

white supremacy, both internally and externally, is a fundamental feminist issue.

For many who came to know about Riot Grrrl in the mid-to-late 1990s, like myself, they were also exposed to critiques of the subculture's whiteness while they learned about the ideals behind "Revolution grrrl style now!" While many of us idealized Riot Grrrl as a movement, we were also more aware of its shortcomings. Zines provided a vital source of education and perspective and served as living examples of critical race theory. Their authors, often young women, used zines as a tool to parse who they were in the world, unapologetically Black, Latina, Asian, Queer, disabled, a white person struggling to be an ally, another calling someone out for not understanding what allyship meant. Zines by writers like Mimi Nguyen, Bianca Ortiz, and Lauren Martin deftly dissected the privilege that was inherent in the movement. Their voices pooled into a river of typewriter ribbons and photocopy toner full of stories. In the late 90s, as I read personal-focused zines that examined race and identity, the name of one zine came up again and again. *Evolution of a Race Riot*, or just "Race Riot" for short, was a compilation zine featuring writers and punks of color edited by Mimi Nguyen. Zinester after zinester attested that it changed their lives and how they saw themselves in terms of race.

"I began this in 1995 at the end of my punk rock love affair," wrote Mimi about *Race Riot*. "I finished it in August 1997 at the beginning of what my best friend calls a multi-subcultural revolution." Mimi, then a graduate student at the University of California at Berkeley, laid it out clearly. "And how much of our time and energy has constantly gone towards whites who demand our attention, our validation, our absolution, our presence as political fetish (monster, mammy, "third world" revolutionary, token)..."[100] Her writing made clear that the "multi-subcultural revolution" was a conversation between and for people of color from different identities.

The essays, stories, comics, and letters in *Evolution of a Race Riot* acted like a counterweight to the rhetoric, or willful silence, around race and racism that permeated my home state of Maine's landscape and popular culture, which was ninety eight percent white, according to the census from the 1980s. A Native American woman recounted how her high school history teacher had tried to claim that "Indians still trade with glass beads." A Latino punk who could pass as white outlined the racist comments his white, punk friends would make in his presence because they didn't think any people of color were around. A Black writer reported that customers at the chain bookstore where she worked only wanted to talk to her about O.J. Simpson. White silence was just another form of complicity that ignored the existence of people like the authors in *Race Riot*. And in the process of becoming aware of that silence and complicities and identifying as "allies," white people could not *demand* that people of color see us as such. As Lauren Martin, who identifies herself as Chinese, Jewish, and queer, from her zine *You Might As Well Live* wrote to white readers, "...and now you can take all that anger and energy and do something positive with it, like educating yourself. Acknowledging your privileges, whatever they may be,

---

100 Mimi Nguyen, Editor, *Evolution of a Race Riot*, published 1997. Available at issuu.com/poczineproject/docs/evolution-of-a-race-riot-issue-1

reading about different cultures and taking the time to listen to other people."

Zines like *Evolution of a Race Riot*, gatherings like New York City's Sista Grrrl Riots organized by Black women, and later James Spooner's 2003 documentary *Afropunk* revealed the limited approach the Riot Grrrl and punk subcultures in general could have to racism. They also demonstrated that punk and hardcore could be a powerful vehicle for community and organizing by people of color, even if they were organizing to push against its prevailing ethos. As Tamar-kali Brown said about being a young, Black, punk woman growing up in New York City, "I was just like, 'I have to survive. I have to defend myself.' Riot Grrrl felt really playful, and I wasn't playing."[101] For me as a white teenaged feminist, zines like *Evolution of a Race Riot* served as a living, breathing example and introduction to an expansive, liberatory approach to intersectional feminism. The punk, feminists of color writing these zines brought the ideas of wrtiers like bell hooks, Gloria Anzaldua, and the women of the Combahee River Collective into a contemporary, punk context and showed how feminist theory was informed by the lives that they lived. Zines by women of color showed that personal stories can open us to liberation if we connect our own experiences to the collective. "I care, therefore I critique,"[102] wrote Mimi Nguyen in *Slant 5*. This served as a reminder that critique that deepens and broadens feminism to be more liberatory is work that serves us all.

---

101 Tamar-kali Brown in Bess.
102 Nguyen in Darms, 306.

In the Combahee River Collective statement, cited by many as a key example of intersectional feminism theory and practice, the authors, Black Lesbian Socialist feminists, write, "We believe that the most profound and potentially most radical politics come directly out of our own identities, as opposed to working to end somebody else's oppression… We realize that the liberation of all oppressed peoples necessitates the destruction of the political-economic systems of capitalism and imperialism as well as patriarchy."[103] As the zine writers of color that would come after them, the women of the collective held white women accountable for addressing their own racism, writing, "Eliminating racism in the white women's movement is by definition work for white women to do, but we will continue to speak to and demand accountability on this issue."[104] The message was clear: white people need to own racism as part of themselves and do the work, not lean on people of color to educate or absolve us.

There were also echoes of punk rock attitude in bell hooks' *Feminist Theory from Margin to Center*, when she wrote, "feminism is neither a lifestyle nor a ready-made identity or role one can step into" and "racist stereotypes of the strong, superhuman black woman are operative myths in the minds of many white women."[105] Like the punks and Riot Grrrls of *Race Riot* and the Combahee River Collective, writers like hooks stripped away the deflecting decorum, shifting discomfort, and tight-lipped approach to race that I had grown up with in New England. These visionary writers made it clear that a true embrace of feminism

---

103 Combahee River Collective, in *How We Get Free*, Keeanga-Yaamahtta Taylor, Ed. Chicago: Haymarket Books, 2017, 19.
104 Ibid, 27.
105 bell hooks *Feminist Theory from Margin to Center*, Boston: South End Press, 1984, 26.

includes addressing racism because feminism is a politics of liberation for all.

I began college in the fall of 2001 in New York City and, like many Americans, suddenly found myself trying to understand and grapple with a legacy of colonialism and racism on a global scale. In the weeks following 9/11 Islamophobia and Islamaphobic attacks in the US increased—the FBI reported 401 hate crimes that were recorded, including 93 assaults and 296 cases of intimidation against Muslims in 2001, compared to 28 the year before in 2000.[106] This post environment also set a dangerous precedent: The number of assaults against Muslims in the US again surged in 2016 in part due to then candidate-Trump's vitriolic, racist rhetoric.[107]

In New York City my whiteness stood out. In the classroom though, I could spend countless hours trying to parse exactly what white privilege meant, surrounded by mostly white students. This represented a larger demographic trend—despite larger numbers of Black students enrolling in higher education, colleges, especially pricey private schools, still served to reinforce race and class divisions, and the number of Black students on elite campuses has fallen, or remained flat, since 1994.[108] This created an environment that, while diverse, could still center on white students' experiences and discussion and risked tokenizing students of color to be the few or sole representatives of the Black, Latinx, or Asian experience, and where students of color

106 Kuang Keng Kuek Ser, *Date: Hate Crimes Against Muslims Increased After 9/11*, PRI, September 12, 2016. pri.org/stories/2016-09-12/data-hate-crimes-against-muslims-increased-after-911

107 Katayoun Kishi, *Assaults Against Muslims in U.S. Surpass 2001 Level*, Pew Research Center, November 15, 2017, pewresearch.org/fact-tank/2017/11/15/assaults-against-muslims-in-u-s-surpass-2001-level/.

108 theatlantic.com/politics/archive/2015/11/black-college-student-body/417189/

often bore the burden of "educating" white students about the intricacies of racism. Despite our college's "progressive" reputation, both students and professors of color were under pressure from a majority-white administration to prove themselves and their intellectual scholarship, especially as a neoliberal college president tried to increase enrollment and profits. These experiences recalled an essay in *Evolution of a Race Riot* by a woman named Chandra, who exclaimed, "You could not possibly understand what it's like to be a Black woman, or any woman of color for that matter. Don't assume you know everything about blacks or any non-white group because you took a couple of classes in college." Education can't solve everything.

However, education, and creating spaces that reach beyond the often-limiting subculture of punk and Riot Grrrl, can create opportunity for an expansive perspective, deeper learning, and the roots of solidarity to grow. For me that came when I had an opportunity to read Angela Davis' *Women, Race, and Class* freshman year and then see her speak. A figure venerated in punk zines and activist circles, known mostly for her iconic Afro and raised fist, it was only thanks to our class syllabus that I realized she had published books that I could actually read. White punks, even if they were devotedly anti-racist, often reduced people of color to overly simplistic symbols. Davis' scholarship and activism is both wide ranging and tightly focused on the intersections of race, gender, class, and social justice. In *Women, Race, and Class*, published in 1981, she examines how racism, slavery, and capitalism fueled white and Black constructions of feminity and slavery, while her later work has focused on prison abolition and the role of prisons under capitalism. In 2001, when she spoke about the ways the prison and military-industrial complexes were woven together in the US, I realized that the fetish-like nostalgia of Davis, the Black Panthers, and armed revolution that my punk friends had held up as the be-all and end-all of radicalism also cast the movement's struggles in amber. I thought about the groups I had been a part of when I lived in Portland, Oregon, and how we had been obsessed with the *image* of resistance that activists like Davis stood for without fully understanding the historical context they were operating in. Activists like Davis herself showed how the struggle to end racism, and oppression in all its forms, is lifelong and depends on personal, and collective, evolution.

For those involved in punk and Riot Grrrl, we had longed for revolution, but we looked past the activism that was already taking place in the communities where we lived, and that prevented us from trying to connect with communities very different from our own. Our idealized dreams of a specific kind of revolution caused us to overlook organizing that we may not have deemed sexy, but pursued a longer term vision of justice. I saw why, through idealizing individuals like Davis, we created unrealistic and unsustainable ideas about what radical activism and solidarity with people of color looked like, and why punk-driven organizing often faltered. Punks, Riot Grrrls, and all activists need the perspective of people like Davis, who have been in the struggle for decades, to help us understand the present. That fall and winter, as Bush threatened deportation of Muslims and mass arrests of anyone thought to be aiding terrorists, Davis' understanding of the ways colonialism, racism, and the legacy of slavery worked together to create contemporary oppression was, and is, as relevant as ever.

Speaking with Davis that day was also Mab Segrest, whose book *Memoir of a Race Traitor* describes her experience living the South as an out lesbian in the 1970s and organizing against the far right and the Klu Klux Klan in North Carolina in the 80s. The book details how she defied her family's commitment to segregation and deep seated racism to stand up and organize against white supremacy as a queer woman in the deep South. In the conclusion she states,

> As a child of Europeans, a woman whose families have spent many generations on these shores, some of them in relative material privilege, my culture raised me to compete: for grades, for jobs, for money, for self-esteem. As my lungs breathed in competition, they breathed out the stale air of individualism... Traveling across race and class and cultural boundaries, my ear eventually became tuned to different vibrations so that I began to hear, first as a murmur, then as a clearly articulated sound: *We... are...in...this...together.*[109]

Segrest's writing about coming to terms with her own whiteness and her commitment to activism had a distinctly different tone than white Riot Grrrls centering themselves. She outlined not only how white entitlement is a dangerous lie, but that white people can and must commit to ending racism through acknowledging their role in perpetuating it and engaging in tangible organizing work if they are to claim "solidarity" or "allyship" with people of color. Being an imperfect ally, Segrest illustrates, must not stop white people from doing the work of

---

109 Mab Segrest *Memoir of a Race Traitor,* Boston: South End Press, 1994, 174.

anti-racism. Transnational feminist M. Jacqui Alexander also spoke to this idea in introductory remarks at a panel celebrating the release of the book *This Bridge We Call Home*, a tribute to the groundbreaking anthology *This Bridge Called My Back*. She said, "We must reach into ourselves, probe the hidden places within us, and look at them in political context."

Cultivating anti-racist activism and consciousness is a lifelong process. However, within subcultures like Riot Grrrl, and activism more broadly, white women often were vying to be the most radical and the most anti-racist. As I tried to weave together my Riot Grrrl-inflected feminism into a more expansive, global anti-racist perspective, I often practiced my allyship with a brittle, studious perfectionism. Younger white people who are coming to consciousness often express similar sentiments, often through the very public lens of social media. It's as if life is another college course where we are striving to get As. This is another way whiteness functions—to create competition and a drive for perfectionism where there should be mutual understanding, thoughtful critique, passionate transformation, and a commitment to self-awareness and constant evolution. In introducing *This Bridge We Call Home*, Alexander invited those gathered to hear her to look at how factionalism tears apart movements and relationships, especially between women, and how finding solidarity is different than silencing difference. These kinds of tensions had torn through the Riot Grrrl movement. Some girls thought it should be connected to larger struggles for social and racial justice, and others thought the concept of "grrrl love" should erase differences and tensions between women, which served to continue to center white women's experiences.

Alexander reminded her listeners that, if we were committed to social justice, we could also be committed to growing with each other while taking responsibility for our own actions, noting, "We must not brand those who make a mistake or display short-sightedness as evil. And we must use our mistakes as moments to grow and heal."

During the winter of 2003, while President Bush's hawkish rhetoric around punishing "evildoers" pushed the world towards war with Iraq, one question seemed central: how to combat this racist madness? Like *Evolution of a Race Riot* years earlier, another zine anthology that centered the voices of people of color in punk-affiliated subcultures offered a framework for healing. *Letters From the War Years*, which was described by its editor, Leah Lakshmi Piepzna-Samarasinha (a mixed-race Sri Lankan queer woman), as a "queer/trans, people of color, anti-war zine." Leah had been influenced early on by the punk and Riot Grrrl movements, but had also soon grown past them, writing in her zine in the late 1990s, "I left Riot Grrrl behind because it could not grow with the questions we were asking of it. It was a movement founded in the ideas that girl love can save the world... which it can't... but I will always remain grateful to grrrl-punk and zine culture for teaching me to speak the truth, love my freakishness and make my own freedom."[110] Leah described Riot Grrrl as a launch pad, a first step, something that started her on her journey to living a radical life attuned to justice, but made it clear that she didn't need to stay within the boundaries of punk to grow into the radical life she envisioned for herself.

---

110 Leah Lakshmi Piepzna-Samarasinha, "Sticks and Stones May Break My Bones," in *A Girl's Guide to Taking Over the World*, Karen Green and Tristan Taormino, eds. New York: St. Martin's Griffin, 1997, 4.

In *Letters From the War Years*, Leah painted a picture of solidarity that blended a punk, DIY sensibility with a global, intersectional perspective and anti-imperialist analysis. She wrote about her friends of color who were "Forming all POC squads to march in the protests, making anti war stickers and going out and slapping them all over Brooklyn, making bomb ass poetry and writing in the face of death and fascism... They were doing activism on their own terms. Creating our own space as queers, trans folks, people of color and Indigenous folks, broke-ass folks, disabled folx, immigrants and 'illegal' folks—making our resistance in our image. Taking care of each other like we need to be."

The second term of the Bush presidency felt like the ultimate fantasy of American whiteness come to life: a knee-jerk patriotism at the expense of people of color, Muslims, the LGBTQ community, and anyone who was pro-choice. Trump's election a decade later would take this even further. The question of how to confront the danger of white supremacy seemed ever more urgent. Mab Segrest had shown one model with her work in the South against racist violence and demonstrated the responsibility white people could take on in deeply supporting communities of resistance that were led by people of color. In *Notes of a Native Son* James Baldwin also captures and hones that responsibility in scorching prose, "The people who think of themselves as White have the choice of becoming human or irrelevant... Or—as they are, indeed, already, in all but actual fact: obsolete."[111] Baldwin insisted that the power that whiteness claims as its own can't last. Ta-Nehisi Coates echoes Baldwin's searing observations about

111 James Baldwin, *Notes of a Native Son*, Boston: Beacon Press, 1984, p. xv.

white, willed, ignorant innocence. He writes, "[White people] have forgotten the scale of the theft that enriched them in slavery; the terror that allowed them, for a century, to pilfer the vote; the segregationist policy that gave them their suburbs ... I am convinced that [they] would rather live white than live free."[112] It's this collective forgetting that enables many white people to believe that the advantages they experience in society they have earned on their own merit and the same sentiment that drove some white women involved in Riot Grrrl to think that being critical of their own racism wasn't applicable to practicing "Grrrl love."

Baldwin, along with writers and activists like Davis, Segrest, and the Black feminists that made up the Combahee River Collective, showed that artists, writers, and activists engaged with social justice have a responsibility to constantly interrogate and illuminate systems of power in society and assess our place within them. As a white person I was raised to view whiteness as neutral, objective, and standard—the default setting of American culture. The authors and thinkers and activists I encountered, first within punk and then beyond, shattered all of that and pushed me to understand that simple-yet-difficult-for-white-people-to-grasp idea that any belief in white superiority and separateness is not only a toxic, dangerous fallacy, but damaging to all of us. Historian Derrick Bell neatly disassembled this logic of white people rightfully earning all that they have. He writes, "The slavery compromises set a precedent under which black rights have been sacrificed throughout the nation's history to further white

---

112 Ta-Nehisi Coates *Between The World and Me*, New York: Spiegel & Grau, 2015, 143.

interests. Those compromises are far more than an embarrassing blot on our national history. Rather they are the original and still definitive examples of the ongoing struggle between individual rights reform and the maintenance of the socio economic status quo."[113] As Bell points out, inequality has been ensconced into the United States' structure and Black subjugation, first through slavery and then through suppression of rights and access to education, housing, and jobs that continue to the present day and directly contribute to how white femininity has been conceived and constructed in the United States.

What my education, both at college and in the Riot Grrrl, zine, and activist communities, offered me was the ability to question the structure of power and see through the lens of race at the intersection of gender, class, and sexuality. I also learned to look for communities and ideas beyond the scope of punk. However, I found the personal, do-it-yourself spirit that was embodied in the Riot Grrrl movement as I encountered it equipped me to be crucial to assessing and understanding racism and the dangers of whiteness as a white person. While you can't "do it yourself" out of institutionalized oppression, I learned that I didn't have to wait for an external answer or solution to addressing power, privilege, and oppression within my own life. For me that has taken many different forms including writing curriculum and co-teaching courses at museums that used art to facilitate questions around race and representation, working for greater diversity and inclusion in the tech industry, and working with my neighbors to host free legal clinics for undocumented immigrants in our

113 Derrick Bell *White Superiority in America: Its Legal Legacy, Its Economic Costs*, published in *Black on White*, edited by David R. Roediger, New York, Shocken Books, 1998, 139.

Brooklyn neighborhood. White women specifically have much reckoning to do about how they historically and presently benefit from and perpetuate institutionalized racism, especially as 45% of white women voted for Donald Trump in 2016[114] and between 45 and 55% of white women voted for him in 2020, depending on the data set[115].

Being pushed to think more deeply about racism and white supremacy through reading zines by Riot Grrrls, punks, and feminists of color, and then later well known theorists and writers, taught me a few simple lessons that I've applied in my life over and over again to keep learning and growing as an ally. They are:

- Do your own work: Reflect on your own life and examine your assumptions about race and identity—share and discuss it, but refrain from centering yourself.

- Show up for people and communities of color in ways they invite and ask you to as a white person. Show up to be of service and because we are in this fight against racism and white supremacy together, not to assuage your ego and insecurity.

- Drop the idea of perfectionism—you will make "mistakes." Learn to sit with discomfort and think about why you feel that way.

114 Pew Research Center, *An examination of the 2016 electorate, based on validated voters*, August 9, 2018, people-press.org/2018/08/09/an-examination-of-the-2016-electorate-based-on-validated-voters/. Accessed on March 23, 2020.
115 Angelina Chapin, *Of Course White Women Voted for Trump Again*, The Cut, November 17, 2020, thecut.com/2020/11/many-white-women-still-voted-for-trump-in-2020.html. Accessed on January 31, 2021.

- Expand your idea of what an "activist" can look like—the actions you take will change as you grow and as the political context in which we live evolves. You don't have to be the most militant or radical person to act in solidarity.

Movements like Black Lives Matter, led by three queer women and expanded exponentially around the globe, have brought mainstream awareness of how state sanctioned, racist violence operates within the United States. They have also highlighted the importance of white people acting in solidarity and addressing racism in their own communities and lives because without serious, wide-spread investment by other white people in countering white supremacy, its legacy will continue in the United States. This is a philosophy also espoused and used as an organizing principle for groups like Showing Up for Racial Justice (SURJ). It has taken writers and activists of color tremendous work to do what should be so simple: convince white people to stand for justice and fight for real equity.

As a result of these grassroots, community-driven movements, intersectionality and solidarity and tributes to the organizing done in communities of color is often given a nod in mainstream feminism. But similar to zines, it's not just talking about it on social media or in "think pieces," but showing up and embodying a feminist politics that advocates for liberation for all. This is a tenet of the Combahee River Collective's statement, and places issues such as prison abolition and ending police violence in communities of color and ending detention of immigrants at its center. As the Combahee River Collective wrote, "If Black women were free, it would mean everyone else would have to be free since our freedom would necessitate the destruction of all the systems of oppression."[116] Because discrimination is pernicious and constant, and power works to limit all of our lives, even those of us who benefit, it's imperative for those with privilege to continusouly be aware of, and raise questions about, power and privilege in our communities. The work to end white supremacy must seep into all aspects of our lives.

116 Keeanga-Yamahtta Taylor, Ed. *How We Get Free: Black Feminism and the Combahee River Collective*, Chicago: Haymarket Books, 2017, 20.

ACTIVISM BEGINS AT HOME
Creating Space

"*A mo a mis vecinos inmigrantes*," proclaimed my hastily painted pink block letters on dark blue poster board. "I love my immigrant neighbors." I grabbed it and ran out the door into the late fall afternoon to the Sunset Park Unity March, the paint wet, hoping that Google translate wasn't too far off.

I met the march coming up the hill through the park, a giant puppet of the Statue of Liberty leading the way, a mixture of Mexican, Chinese, Central American, and white families and activists, a cross section of the neighborhood. I merged into the crowd, and we marched down Fifth Avenue, past bodegas and discount housewares stores, sidewalk stands selling *gorditas* and *empanadas*, the traffic slow with Sunday shoppers. Cars full of Mexican families and riders on the city bus wearing headscarves smiled, honked, and waved as we marched by chanting, "Love! Not Hate! Makes America Great!" While the message was simple, fulfilling the ideas behind it would not be, but as I marched I felt the fog of grief that had hung over me for the month since the 2016 presidential election lift and muscle memory from years of organizing kick in. I felt like I had come home.

Like many who "discover" activism, I first came to it as a teenager informed by a personal experience of injustice, a burning desire to "change the world," and a determination to advance my new-found feminism by every means necessary. An emotionally abusive relationship with my high school boyfriend acted as a catalyst that pushed me into discovering who I was as a feminist.

For me, feminist activism was a path towards healing and a way to express my rage. I connected with a local group that helped teenagers address dating and domestic violence and, simultaneously, discovered the feminist punk of Riot Grrrl. The realization that everyday people had the power to challenge the status quo, actively work together for a new reality, and didn't need to wait for permission to be the people we wanted to be, was heady.

Protest is a tactic to make private rage public and connect personal injustice to larger social issues. During one of the first protest actions in which I participated, in the late 1990s, I stood resolute with other teenagers on the brick sidewalk in Portland, Maine, as rush hour traffic flowed by. We held signs with the names and photos of recent victims of domestic violence printed on them, incensed that young women between 18 and 24 were the most commonly abused by their partners and that, in Maine, domestic violence comprised a majority of homicides.[117] We came out to a particular intersection to protest every time someone in the state was killed by a violent partner, which was often several times a month, and in the year I was involved the victims were always women. It was a stark reminder of what we were up against and the stakes of injustice.

When one first begins to understand how forces of power and privilege intersected to shape the world, just seeing injustice everywhere can feel like a revelation. Resistance can also be found everywhere and every small act of resistance is like a mini-

---

117 National Coalition Against Domestic Violence, "Domestic Violence in Maine," accessed on September 9, 2019, speakcdn.com/assets/2497/maine.pdf.

revolution. This kind of right-here, right-now resistance was part of what was appealing for young people involved in and inspired by Riot Grrrl. For Riot Grrrls and those influenced by them, that could be raising awareness about upcoming legislation that would impact reproductive rights, educating peers on safe, consensual sex, supporting other young people organizing benefit shows and protest actions, reading zines by and writing letters to other young feminists to build community, booking feminist bands and organizing feminist events, and seeking out books, movies, and articles to educate ourselves on intersectional feminism. Personally I hoped that engaging in practices like these would add up to being a feminist and each quoditian act would bring the world one step closer to a feminist revolution and the eradication of sexism once and for all. However, these small acts cannot stay at the individual level. To create social change, they must connect to larger movements.

Activists are often cited as wanting to "change the world," but this can come off as self-centered and self-involved. Taking up activism also asks the question of "how do you enact your values in the world and put yourself in the service of social justice?" which is a more nuanced question. DIY values, like those espoused by punk and Riot Grrrl, can help activists identify and connect with local issues that are close to home that they can have a direct effect on changing. However, a potential pitfall of these values are that those who subscribe to them focus on the "yourself" part and think of activism as something that needs to not only be right here, right now, but also yield immediate results.

Activism is a long game with unpredictable results. In protest there's often a dichotomy: to act with a clear message and goal in mind while understanding that even if that goal was far from being achieved, the action is still meaningful and can have consequences beyond what you initially expect. For example, "The World Says No to War" on February 15, 2003 consisted of over 600 coordinated anti-war rallies throughout the world protesting Bush's war on Iraq, including a record-breaking 3 million people protesting in Rome. Scholars and journalists called it the largest single-day protest event in human history.[118] After months of energetic organizing, and millions of calls to elected officials, Bush pushed ahead with his invasion of Iraq and stepped up deportations of immigrants in the United States. Bush's decision sent a wave of heartbreak, anger, and defeat through activist communities at the time, and many declared that the protests had "failed," a view and feeling I shared for many years.

Rebecca Solnit reflected on the protests against the Iraq war, writing, "The despairing could only recognize victory, the one we didn't grasp, the prevention of the war in Iraq."[119] She goes on to discuss the more subtle victories: the engagement of a diverse range of "everyday" people in politics and civic life, putting the war up for debate and making a strong point that Bush and his cronies couldn't alone decide the fate of the world, and a strengthening of communities and coalition building that would last beyond the protests. It also went on to fuel future organizing such as Occupy Wall Street and, indirectly, Black Lives Matter.

---

118 Stefaan Walgrave and Dieter Rucht, Eds. The World Says No to War, (Minneapolis, University of Minnesota press, 2010), xiii.
119 Rebecca Solnit, Hope in the Dark, (Haymarket Books, Chicago, 2016), 14.

Especially coming from a punk perspective, where many want to have an immediate and tangible impact on the world, it was hard for me and many activists to embrace a perspective like Solnit's at the time. The events that followed added to the sense of leaden despair that hung in the air: the abuses in Abu Ghraib and Guantanamo Bay, the detentions of Muslim immigrants in New York and New Jersey, cuts to public education, abstinence only sex education, drilling in the arctic, came one after another, policy after policy designed to advance a cruel, power hungry agenda at the expense of the vulnerable.

To be an activist means to hold a macro understanding of the challenges and injustices that are shaping society and to understand how they manifest on a personal and local level. It's to live by that old adage, often attributed to the environmental movement in the 1970s, to "think globally and act locally." The question of why we act is also important: do we act out of our own sense of power, or to make up for our perceived sense of powerlessness? When activism comes from a place of perfectionism and fear that you will never be enough, it's difficult to push past your own inertia and really open yourself to acting in solidarity with impacted communities. Activism and organizing can take many forms, from addressing global politics to confronting issues that directly support our local communities.

In my early twenties I chose to focus my organizing energy on a space I knew well: the zine community. I helped found and organize the Portland Zine Symposium, which was trying to make a space for community building between independent artists and zine and comics publishers. Spaces like this can ease a collective sense of hopelessness and help chase away the weighty feeling of political despair. However, if we approach activism with a mindset that only considers it "successful" if it achieves a specific, political outcome they can seem frivolous and self-indulgent. This attitude also treats radical spaces as separate from our society, when often they are simply a specific microcosm and not immune to larger structures of power.

In the summer of 2003 we were getting ready for that summer's symposium when a well-known zine writer, editor, and event organizer was accused of multiple instances of sexual assault. He had attended the symposium in the past and we felt we had committed a collective act of unseeing by not being more aware of his oppressive behavior. As organizers we wanted to ensure he did not attend and that we addressed the underlying issues, which would mean pushing the zine community to recognize some ugly behavior that many people wanted to believe we were above and beyond. While many of us who were part of the punk and zine making communities identified ourselves as staunch feminists, we did not have a well-articulated strategy to deal with issues related to sexual assault directly. Strategies for addressing sexual assault in the punk community had ranged from photocopied fliers, passed around and reproduced in zines that outed certain men in bands as rapists, facts shared through "whisper networks" about questionable punk men, and confessional pieces in zines and tearful sessions at Riot Grrrl conventions and zine gatherings about the impact of sexual assault on survivors. While some Riot Grrrls and zine makers were involved in the reproductive freedom and justice and anti-sexual violence movements, the two were not always connected. As organizers we did not feel fully equipped to fashion a coherent, thoughtful response that would create a change not only at our event, but in the culture as a whole.

One strategy we employed was to create a collective code of conduct, defining where we stood on assault, discrimination, and harassment, outlining expectations for everyone attending the symposium and explicitly outlining that those not adhering to them would be asked to leave. Writer and computer programmer Ashe Dryden states that a Code of Conduct simply, "lays the ground rules and notifies both bad actors as well as the people at the receiving end of that behavior that there are consequences for those actions."[120] While these have become de rigueur for conferences, workplaces, and activist gatherings, in 2004 to have a Code of Conduct was still a radical idea. Participants that carried more societal privilege often assumed that a shared interest in "alternative" culture or radical politics was enough to ensure everyone would act "cool" and that assault, harassment, and discrimination were only perpetuated by "bad" and "ignorant" people. However, as the more recent #MeToo movement has demonstrated to the mainstream, assault is a widespread issue perpetuated by those we know and often love. Over 320,000 assaults occur in the US each year,[121] and only about one fourth of them are reported.[122] In a society full of explicit discrimination, measures to counter it must also be explicit.

The community that attended the symposium was a loose network of people who had decided to reject, or been rejected

120 Ashe Dryden, "Code of Conduct 101," February 10, 2014, accessed on September 14, 2019, ashedryden.com/blog/codes-of-conduct-101-faq.
121 RAINN, "Scope of the Problem: Statistics," accessed on September 14, 2019, rainn.org/statistics/scope-problem.
122 Ibid, "The Criminal Justice System: Statistics," rainn.org/statistics/criminal-justice-system.

by, mainstream culture, values, and spaces to some degree who wanted to focus on creating their own subversive spaces. Like many radical and alternative spaces, what made this loose network of people strong in terms of creativity and resistance also made it challenging when it came to speaking up against discrimination, sexual assault, and harassment. Community members had found each other because we did not conform and were often skeptical, if not downright opposed, to getting government agencies or any kind of "authorities" or "professionals" involved in community issues. However, this also assumed that alternative communities were somehow isolated from larger societal issues, which made us less capable of addressing them and achieving our vision for a more equitable world.

One of the more experienced symposium organizers, a woman who had been in the Portland punk community for many years, rightly suggested we bring in an outside, professional facilitator to run a workshop about combatting and healing from sexual assault and to help guide our policies. While punks may have bristled at this kind of "outside" intervention, it also helped connect our underground fathering to larger issues and perspectives. Building true solidarity and connecting events and workshops to larger issues around social justice took time, planning, and careful facilitation. Taking consistent, small steps are what can shift culture over time.

Creating the spaces that enable cultural transformation, and who is asked to maintain those spaces and ensure they are inclusive, welcoming, and well organized, is often seen as "behind the scenes" work. As a result, it often falls to women, people of color, and those with less societal privilege, while at the same time, doesn't always get recognized as activism in the same way organizing visible demonstrations, campaigns, or legislative actions might. This dichotomy was illustrated to me all too well when a zine maker who had worked organizing steel workers in the midwest and participating in demonstrations with Black Bloc anarchists informed me that organizing people and organizing events were different and that "Events serve a certain, self-defined political community. They do not advance political change." Readings, exhibits at museums and galleries, punk shows, lectures and panel discussions, and workshops didn't fit in the category of "organizing people" but can have life changing and movement building results. These are the places where community and relationships are strengthened and knowledge about issues and causes broadened and deepened.

So many initiatives that have created a lasting legacy of social justice are tied to creating cultural space as a springboard for change. Kitchen Table: Women of Color Press, started by Barbarbara Smith and Audre Lorde and other Black feminists in 1980, published works by authors like bell hooks and the groundbreaking anthology *This Bridge Called My Back: Writings of Radical Women of Color,* edited by Cherie Moraga and Gloria Anzaldua. Books like these centered the voices of women of color within feminism and laid the foundation for the modern, widespread embrace of intersectional feminism. The importance of culture and its relationship to revolutionary change was embodied in the name of press. As Barbara Smith wrote, "We chose our name because the kitchen is the center of the home, the place where women in particular communicate with each other. We also wanted to convey the fact we are a kitchen table, a grassroots operation, begun and kept alive by women who cannot rely on inheritances or other benefits of class privilege to do the work we need to do."[123] The women who created Kitchen Table approached it as both a literary and activist project, one that served to build community, raise awareness, and address sexism, heterosexism, and all forms of oppression in activist and communities of color and beyond.

"The personal is political" was made famous by feminist activists in the sixties and seventies. This idea had been crucial for enabling women to connect their individual experiences of oppression, whether that be domestic violence at home, sexual harassment at work, coming out as a lesbian, or their experience of racism as a woman of color, to a collective identity and movement that worked, imperfectly, to dismantle systems of oppression as a whole. Cultural Studies as an academic field of study conceded space to analyzing and celebrating the abilities of an individual or communities to act in the world on their own terms, to generate their own meanings, and develop their own uses for cultural products as well as resistance to oppression.[124] Personally, I was invested in the idea that culture could be resistance. It was the same impulse that drove me, as a teenager influenced by the punk and Riot Grrrl movements, to write personal essays about my experiences and share them with other young women across the country through zines. To assume there is not a "cultural" element to organizing assumes a kind of dangerous neutrality

123 Smith, Barbara. "A Press of Our Own Kitchen Table: Women of Color Press." *Frontiers: A Journal of Women Studies* 10, no. 3 (1989): 11-13. doi:10.2307/3346433.
124 Simon During, ed. *The Cultural Studies Reader,* London: Routledge, 2003, 6.

that could also be attributed to whiteness. To focus on shared culture, traditions, language, and experiences of oppression, and to know yourself, your community, and your issues, is how movements are built.

"Cultural" and "political" organizing are not a dichotomy, but essential parts of creating change overall. Some activists try to outdo each other by being more "radical" or rigidly enforce a "correct" way to be an activist. Doing so can lead to burnout, despair, and detachment. When we don't use our talents because we don't think they fit into this narrow spectrum of "activism," we deny the skills we have to connect with others and the world as a whole. Cultural organizing and creating space for learning, community building, and empowerment challenges rigid perfection and activist orthodoxy and creates capacity for possibility.

Power Together

"Wine?" asked Chitra, the host of our neighborhood organizing meeting, as soon as I walked into her Brooklyn kitchen in November of 2016. I had half expected to walk back into the activist potlucks of Portland, Oregon circa 2000, complete with gluey vegan macaroni and cheese made with nutritional yeast, cups of warm Santa Cruz organic lemonade, and the vague smell of body odor permeating throughout. Those gatherings, held in punk houses and community spaces, had been culturally homogenous, and majority white.

While we often acknowledged our "privilege" in those spaces, as young activists coming from mostly white, middle class backgrounds we were struggling to understand how to put our desire to stand in solidarity with more diverse communities into action. Our homes were the spaces we used to organize and build community because they were what we could afford, they were an oasis of punk culture, and we had little idea how to access or be part of spaces beyond those that were predefined as punk or anarchist.

The meeting at my neighbor's house in 2016 was distinctly different. It was a starting point for building a very local practice of solidarity between those with economic and racial privilege and those with less, to support those who were the most vulnerable under Trump's presidential administration. Meetings like this were a groundswell of activism driven by women around the country that took on voter registration and education, fundraising for political candidates, and running for office. In my local group alone, at least five of the thirty-or-so of us had been involved in punk and Riot Grrrl. There we found we could channel skills first formed organizing punk shows and publishing zines and further honed by our experiences as academics, professionals, and parents into wider looking community change. Following the presidential election in 2016 journalist Rebecca Traistor observed, "In special elections and primary campaigns, newly angry women brought skills they'd learned in the PTA to canvassing and organizing."[125] Of course, many of us had long been angry and long been organizing, especially women of color

125 Rebecca Traistor, *Good and Mad: The Revolutionary Power of Women's Anger*, (New York, Simon and Schuster, 2018), 212.

in lower income communities, but the post-election environment gave a broad range of women an opportunity and a clarion call to recognize a range of shared issues and begin to figure out how to organize around them.

The international reach of the first Women's March, held the day after Trump's inauguration in 2017, was the largest single-day protest event recorded in US history and captured much media attention. However, grassroots activists around the country were focused and motivated by what we could do to resist the Trump agenda on a local level, taking cues from local activism, electoral politics, and intersectional feminism. The months after Trump's election and inauguration felt open and unpredictable. As a result, actions around the country were wide-ranging, creative, and experimental. Postcards and phone calls to representatives flowed in. Town hall attendance bulged. Thousands showed up at airports and marched to protest Trump's "Muslim ban," an executive order banning entry to the US from travelers from Iran, Iraq, Libya, Somalia, Sudan, Syria, and Yemen, separating families and illustrating the racism and cruelty that would come to define the administration. There was a need to make ideas like solidarity and allyship, that could sometimes seem abstract for those with race and class privilege, tangible.

The phrase "the resistance" has a nice, Star-Wars-esque ring to it, but it is also vague. The term has come to encompass everything from political postcard writing, to running for office and supporting progressive candidates, to learning about bystander intervention, to radical, direct action like blocking ICE vehicles to prevent deportations. With Trump out of office, its momentum may sputter as there is not a coherent political force to "resist." However, systematic oppression continues and within the umbrella term of "the resistance" there is a greater ability to start where you are as an activist and a greater acceptance of the broadness of activist possibilities than were in the punk activist community. There are many ways in and just because you start with one kind of action, like calling your representatives, doesn't mean you won't move into others, like volunteering for a progressive candidate, escorting at an abortion clinic, or organizing and participating in direct actions and protests. The key, however, is to take action of some kind, learn, reflect, and keep going.

One key action my neighborhood "resistance" group took was to organize monthly Know Your Rights dinners in allies' homes for immigrant families. Hosting these dinners in the homes of allies was a conscious choice not only to build more tangible connections between neighbors of different backgrounds, classes, and citizenship status, but also because many undocuemented people were afraid to come to publicly advertised Know Your Rights seminars, afraid they would be targeted by ICE, and needed confidential, free access to immigration lawyers. It was an act of connecting global needs in the anti-immigrant, white surpemacist climate perpetuated, but certainly not started, by the Trump administration.

Home can be a place to build community and solidarity. Barbara Ehrenreich wrote in *The New York Times* about the changing face of the U.S. working class. She described making chili and hosting picnics for union leaders and local labor organizers at her home in 1980s Long Island. Her social circle is now long gone, as are the union factory jobs that anchored it, but she reflected on the type of organizing she and her friends supported. "As a group, we had no particular ideology, but our vision, which was articulated through our parties rather than any manifesto, was utopian... it could be summed up in the old-fashioned word 'solidarity': If you join my picket line, I'll join yours... We wanted a world in which everyone's work was honored and every voice heard."[126] Sharing my home as a base for organizing was a small way to use what I had to contribute to a collective push for a more just political future. That old-fashioned idea of "solidarity" that Ehrenreich discussed and I had yearned for as a young activist and punk now seemed within reach. Solidarity is not an abstract idea, but an evolving, ever changing practice. Events, parties, and picnics, as Ehrenreich explains, can be places to build and sustain a movement. However, between the Bush years and Trump's election, the divide in my mind between cultural events and "real" organizing had become uncrossable. Burnout, overwhelm, and insecurity had also been a factor in not being able to see a way forward as an activist that resonated with who I was. After the Trump election, I, along with many other women who came of age in the 1990s, rediscovered or found their way to a multifaceted approach to activism starting very much in our own experiences and community, just as we had done as Riot Grrrls.

In *Hope in the Dark*, her little black book of the resistance that was originally published during the Bush era, Rebecca Solnit writes,

126 nytimes.com/2017/02/23/magazine/american-working-class-future.html

"Hope and action feed each other... When I think back to why I was apolitical in my mid-twenties I see that being politically engaged means having a sense of your own power—that what you do matters—and a sense of belonging, things that came to me later and that do not come to all. Overcoming alienation and isolation or their causes is a political goal for the rest of us. And for the rest of us, despair is an indulgence if you look at the power for being political as a privilege not granted to everyone."[127]

Home, in a concrete sense as well as in our communities, cities, and towns, is a place where collective power can be cultivated. There is not a gap between building community and building political power—they are intimately tied together. Organizing with my neighborhood group took us into homes, churches, community centers, public parks, and elementary schools for meetings, free legal clinics, workshops, and information sharing. These places are everyday, intimate, and worn with the familiar. In them, women from many different class backgrounds and immigration statuses take the lead, as PTA heads, fundraisers, and event organizers have laid the groundwork for us to tap into our community power in a crucial political moment.

Building power in community can enable nimble growth and changes as new crises arise and politics continue to evolve. Taking a DIY approach to organizing doesn't mean having to have an answer to "fix" systemic oppression, but making an impact with the resources available to you and your community and not waiting for permission to jump in to marshall those to

127 Rebecca Solnit, *Hope in the Dark*, Chicago: Haymarket Books, 2016, 12.

protect more vulnerable neighbors. In my neighborhood that evolution has looked like "ICE watches" when the agency began targeting families there with raids in 2019, a mutual aid group that distributes groceries, household necessities, and financial, logistical, and material support, protesting abusive practices by law enforcement at a local detention center, and organizing protests in support of Black Lives Matter throughout 2020. In community we build pockets of resistance, community, safety, and power together. It helps to start with holding space with people who are different from yourself, yet share common concerns and values, acknowledging the differences of power and experience present, and using that awareness to move forward together.

Fostering grassroots community connection can also move into more traditional forms of "political power" and "organizing." While politicians, policy makers, and political commentators expressed skepticism that local movements led by women and people of color would translate into "hard" power, the 2018 elections proved their sexist dismissal wrong. In New York State local organizing led to throwing regressive Democrats who voted on Republican lines out of the State Senate, and cleared the way for laws championed by grassroots activists that protected women's, immigrants', and housing rights to pass. Nationally, as has been well documented, in 2018 a record 125 women won House, Senate, or gubernatorial positions, buoyed by a broadly activated local base of supporters.[128] While some of those seats were lost again in 2020, an activated and more radical base of Democratic voters, whether they belong to the party or not,

128 "The Women Rule Candidate Tracker," Politico, accessed October 5, 2019, politico.com/interactives/2018/women-rule-candidate-tracker/.

champion feminist values and are gathering political experience to be a force to shape national conversations around social justice and equality for years to come.

While organizing with a local lens with a long view of social justice and social change may not ring with the clarion call of "revolution girl style now," it does mesh with the do-it-yourself, accessibility, and immediacy that drew many to punk and Riot Grrrl in the first place. When smaller, local actions are driven by a radical, expansive vision they can reach concretely towards larger change. Overcoming perfectionism and burnout in activism means shifting focus. It means holding a "both and" mentality: envisioning an expansive future while addressing the present reality. As feminist artist Aurora Lady says, "activism is finding your super power."

Being an activist is not about becoming someone we are not—it's about how we can use our varying strengths and privilege, and enable others to use theirs, to uniquely contribute to a broader movement for justice. Our resistance, nurtured in our homes and in the spaces we create for ourselves, amplified through the culture we build together, must also translate into political power at the policy level and ballot box, as well as restructure how our economy and systems of care are organized. Feminism analysis and action is necessary to address issues as broad as intimate partner violence to discrimination at work to laws that police our bodies and our communities, to politicians who undermine anyone who is not straight, white, cisgendered, and male. A feminist practice rooted in empathy, equity, and solidarity is the connective tissue between intimate spaces, collective organizing, and mass protest.

Our power springs from the stories we tell each other about our lives, in spaces that we make that feel like home. We build a movement through our ability to hear each other, to empathize, to meet at the intersection of identities and experience, to push beyond what we know, and to discover the issues where we connect, to strategize and fight back together. Intersectional feminism is a tool to understand how power flows in society, to hold a multitude of possibilities at once, and to recognize and pursue strategies for organizing and living that have been shut out of the mainstream.

Culture is about power. Politics is about power. Feminism and activism are about making that power collective, sustainable, and available to all, with the wide range of tactics and skills we have available and the ones we have yet to invent. If we can both honor and hold each other accountable, we can grow together in power and feminist resistance.

TOWARDS GIRL UTOPIA

"Your life is good for one thing / You're messing with what's sacred…"

A distorted guitar cut the thick air like a buzzsaw. A woman's voice soared over the crowd and commanded the attention of every ear in the colossal rock club. Her words burst out as raw and urgent as the first time I heard them. I found myself screaming along, their lyrics seared into my memory.

It had been over half of my lifetime since Sleater-Kinney first powered out of my tinny stereo speakers. Watching them, I was back at a basement club in Boston, barely 18, letting their blazing guitars burn life's frustration out of me for a few moments. I remembered the moment I had been pushed against the stage by the sea of girls behind me, all collectively leaning in together, wanting to breathe the same air as Sleater-Kinney and hoping some of their swagger would rub off on us.

Almost two decades later, I was still completely absorbed by the three women on stage. They stomped, swung their detuned guitars with furious confidence, and pounded the drums with an exacting vigor. They seemed like my big sisters or my stylish, rebel aunts who showed me the way forward through my teens and twenties with their riffs, syncopated beats, and perfectly interlaced vocals.

As I hollered along with the massive crowd, most in their 30s and 40s like me, I remembered the excitement of my discovery of feminism, of feeling like every record I listened to and zine I read provided me with more insight about how I could live my life. From those words, sung, written, and spoken, I began to see that life did not have to happen *to me* as a woman, but I could empower myself to chart my own course, discover and build community, and proactively make decisions to shape my life.

As a teenager, feminism had felt like a heady power I could wield. Feminism had felt like a fixed destination, not a process. I had hoped adopting it as a practice would secure me a one-way ticket to girl utopia. I thought that if I could just change the people around me, or go somewhere where the question of feminism was already "answered," I wouldn't have to continuously struggle through life. I didn't realize then that feminism was not a protective spell I could invoke to keep sexism from impacting me. It did not save me from disappointment in myself or other feminist friends and community members, turn me into a wildly successful rock star, a prominent career woman, a famous activist, or give me the gift of naturally egalitarian relationships.

I kept expecting myself to outgrow the ideals that Riot Grrrl-influenced feminism instilled in me and to find a feminist practice that was more definitive and somehow more "adult." While I've grown into a more nuanced understanding of feminism, power, and resistance, the ideas I first encountered through Riot Grrrl still serve me: the importance of finding and nurturing a community; creating spaces for emotion, rage, and for us to be our complete, complex selves; the chance to boldly and loudly call out injustice and oppression and fight against it; to love and celebrate other women and people who do not conform to the status quo; to be critical of the ideals, and ideas, we are handed by our media, politicians, and culture and to reflect on how we might enforce those ourselves; and a do-it-yourself grittiness that values the grassroots and believes in the power of everyday people to create change.

Sexism, racism, homophobia, and the factors that first drew me to the necessity of feminism have not lessened in our society, though they have continued to change form. As an adult in my early-mid-life, these feminist ideas that inspired me as a teenager still serve me when reflecting on how to resist those intertwined forces and build a feminist life. Feminism has given me the ability to keep continuously growing and pushing towards an equitable world, and a staunch belief that it is possible. It did not hand me the key to a perfect, just world, but rather gave a compass or North star by which to navigate the long path to helping create that world.

As I learned from Riot Grrrl, and the feminist thinkers it led me to, intersectional feminism that seeks to understand how our identities, oppressions, and liberations connect is the only way to fully engage the potential of feminism. Feminism is forged in the collective, in enabling formerly marginal voices to take center stage and lead. It is expansive, and as bell hooks asserted in her book of the same name, feminism is for everybody. But to truly create an expansive feminism, we need to ensure we always remain critical of the ways we cling to our own unearned power or privilege, or use it to advance our personal agenda as opposed to collective liberation.

What feminism asks of us is simple: equality and freedom to live and love, and the chance for all to fully realize their potential.

What feminism demands of society is systems and structures that support the liberation and self-actualization for all economically, culturally, and politically. Why would we want anything less? To advance an expansive, intersectional, inclusive version of feminism, we can each commit to and stand for these values daily in private and public ways.

There are so many strategies at our fingertips: listen to and act to support those who are marginalized by patriarchal power; create and champion art and cultural initiatives that help other women; volunteer for and contribute to politicians, organizations, and community groups that put social justice at the center of their agenda; and show up for events, protests, and initiatives organized by and speaking to women of color, queer women, transgender women, and poor and working-class women. Overall, keep questioning the motives of those who hold political and cultural power, build solidarity with those who have experiences beyond your own, and listen to the voice that scratches inside of you when you sense injustice. This is how we will advance feminism and adapt our living, feminist practice.

"When she talks, I hear the revolution / In her hips, there's revolutions / When she walks, the revolution's coming / In her kiss, I taste the revolution!"

Bikini Kill's now iconic call to join the Riot Grrrl revolution and the youthful, idealistic, urgent feminist flame they helped inspire still burns within those of us hungry for change. To commit to the promise of feminism fully is both liberation and a life's labor, but for each of us to reach for and realize that vision would be nothing short of revolution. We can still be our own and each other's rebel grrrls, no matter our age or gender.

I hear the revolution coming and it's within each and everyone of us.

ACKNOWLEDGEMENTS

The process of writing and publication can be genuinely harrowing. Despite over twenty years of spilling my personal stories into zines and sending them out to anyone who might be interested, this creating a book was an exercise in vulnerability.

This book is a small tribute to the many feminist thinkers, groups, activists, teachers, and compatriots who have guided and challenged me along the way, including but not limited to Lauren Martin, Keight Bergmann, Marissa Falco, Felix Endara, Emily North, Ariel Ricci, Lilias Bonechi, Jane Lazarre, Gary Lemons, Amit Rai, Rasmia Kirmani, Emily Kramer, Tracy Candido, Sarah Giovannello, Sarah Sajdak, Marisha Chinsky, Aileen Brophy, Marisa Crawford, Aurora Lady, and Emily Heist Moss.

I am incredibly grateful to all my fellow zine publishers, pen pals, and readers who helped create an intersectional feminist community and dialogue across time, geography, and identity— the impact of your collective and singular words will always stay with me. Thank you especially to the collective projects that I have had the privilege to be a part of: L.I.P.P., the Boston Zine Girl Army, the Radical Art Girls, the Portland Zine Symposium, the New School Free Press, riffRAG, the education division at the Brooklyn Museum, Venus Zine, Weird Sister, and Love Trumps Hate Sunset Park.

A book is so much more than its author. Thank you to all who have nurtured this book since it was barely an idea, especially Elly, Alana, Cyn, Lydia, and Joe at Microcosm Publishing. Thank you to the Sackett Street Writers Workshop, led by Michele Filgate,

Xeni Fragakis, and Jessica Dulong, and my fellow writers who provided invaluable feedback along the way. I could not have finished these essays without the space, time, and community afforded to me by the CAMP residency, and the accountability of my writing group members Lisa Goldstein, Gulshan Mia, Jessie Barker, and Noah Demland. I feel a privilege to be part of the community of writers at the CUNY Queens College MFA program, who keep me growing as a writer. I am so grateful to Marisa Crawford, Krista Suh, Yumi Sakugawa, Emily Gould, and Suzanne Leonard for manuscript review and support!

Personally, thank you to my parents, Mike and Rosemary Whitney. Even if we don't always see eye to eye on the issues, you have always supported my creative work and trusted me to make the best decisions for myself. Thank you Matt Holota for living by his own "death before mansplaining" creed. Special thanks as well to my best feline editorial assistants and writing coaches, Crackers and Biscuit.

But mostly thank you to all of those who identify as feminists and push themselves to fight for justice in big and small ways, who resist oppression and work for liberation with every inch and every breath.

SELECTED BIBLIOGRAPHY AND SUGGESTED FURTHER READING

Ahmed, Sara. *Living a Feminist Life*. Durham, NC: Duke University Press, 2017.

Anzaldua, Gloria. *Borderlands/La Frontera: The New Mestiza*. San Francisco: Aunt Lute Books, 2012 (4th edition).

Anzaldua, Gloria and Cheri Moraga, Eds. *This Bridge Called My Back: Writings by Radical Women of Color*. New York: Kitchen Table Women of Color Press, 1981.

barrera, clare and Meredith Butner, Eds. *When Language Runs Dry: An Anthology for People with Chronic Pain and Their Allies*. Mend My Dress Press, 2020.

Baumgardner, Jennifer and Amy Richards. *Manifesta: Young women, feminism, and the future, 10th anniversary edition*. New York: Farrar, Strauss, and Giroux, 2010.

Baldwin, James. *Notes of a Native Son*, Boston: Beacon Press, 1984.

Bolick, Kate. *Spinster: Making a Life of One's Own*. New York: Crown Publishers, 2015, 15.

brown, adrienne maree. *Emergent Strategy: Shaping change, changing worlds*. Chico, CA: AK Press, 2017.

brown, adrienne maree. *Pleasure Activism: The Politics of Feeling Good*. Chico, CA: AK Press, 2019.

brown, adrienne maree. *We Will Not Cancel Us*. Chico, CA: AK Press, 2020.

Butler, Lisa Gabriel and Cornelia H. Mack, *Wack!: Art and the Feminist Revolution*, Los Angeles: MIT Press, MOCA, 2007.

Coates, Ta-Nehisi. *Between The World and Me*, New York: Spiegel & Grau, 2015.

Collins, Patricia Hill. *Black Feminist Thought: Knowledge, Consciousness, and the Politics of Empowerment*. New York: Routledge, 1991.

Cooper, Brittney. *Eloquent Rage: A Black Feminist Discovers Her Superpower*. New York: St. Martin's Press, 2018.

Darms, Lisa, ed. *The Riot Grrrl Collection*. New York: Feminist Press, 2013.

Davis, Angela. *Women, Race & Class*. New York: Vintage, 1983.

Davis, Angela. *Women, Politics & Culture*. New York: Vintage, (Reprint Edition), 1990.

Davis, Angela. *Freedom Is a Constant Struggle: Ferguson, Palestine, and the Foundations of a Movement*. Chicago: Haymarket Books, 2016.

Eric-Udorie, June. *Can We All Be Feminists? New Writing from Brit Bennett, Nicole Dennis-Benn, and 15 Others on Intersectionality, Identity, and the Way Forward for Feminism*. New York: Penguin Books, 2018.

Feinberg, Leslie. *Trans Liberation: Beyond Pink and Blue*. Boston: Beacon Press, 1998.

Filipovic, Jill Filipovic. *The H-Spot:The Feminist Pursuit of Happiness*. New York: Nation Books, 2017.

Green, Karen and Tristan Taormino, Eds. *A Girl's Guide to Taking Over the World; Writings from the Girl Zine Revolution*. New York: St. Martin's Griffin, 1997.

Hopper, Briallen. *Hard to Love*, New York: Bloomsbury Publishing, 2019.

hooks, bell. *Talking Back: Thinking Feminist, Thinking Black*. New York: Routledge, 2015. First published by South End Press in 1989.

hooks, bell. *Feminism is for Everybody: Passionate Politics*, Boston: South End Press, 2000.

Khan-Cullors, Patricia and Asha Bandele. *When They Call You a Terrorist: A Black Lives Matter Memoir*. New York: St. Martin's Press, 2018.

Lazarre, Jane. *Beyond the Whiteness of Whiteness: Memoir of a White Mother of Black Sons*. Durham, NC: Duke University Press, 1996.

Leonard, Suzanne. *Wife Inc.: The Business of Marriage in the Twenty-First Century*, New York: New York University Press, 2018.

Lippard, Lucy. *From the Center: Feminist Essays on Women's Art*. New York: E.P. Dutton & Co., Inc., 1976.

Lorde, Audre. *Sister Outsider*. New York: Ten Speed Press, 1984.

Marcus, Sara. *Girls to the Front: The True Story of the Riot Grrrl Revolution*. New York: Harper Perennial, 2010.

McRobbie, Angela. *The Aftermath of Feminism: Gender, Cultural, and Social Change,* London: Sage, 2009.

Odell, Jenny. *How to Nothing: Resisting the Attention Economy,* New York: Melville House, 2019.

Oluo, Ijeoma. *So You Want to Talk About Race,* New York: Seal Press, 2019.

Piepzna-Samarasinha, Leah Lakshmi. *Care Work: Dreaming Disability Justice*. Vancouver: Arsenal Pulp Press, 2018.

Reilly, Maura and Linda Nochlin. *Global Feminisms: New Directions in Contemporary Art,* New York: Merrell Publishers, 2007.

Rothblum, Esther and Sondra Solovay, eds. *The Fat Studies Reader,* New York: New York University Press, 2009.

Schaefer, Kayleen. *Text Me When You Get Home,* New York: Dutton, 2018

Schulman, Sarah. *Ties That Bind: Familial Homophobia and Its Consequences*. New York: The New Press, 2009.

Segrest, Mab. *Memoir of a Race Traitor,* Boston: South End Press, 1994.

Sollee, Kristen J. *Witches, Sluts, Feminists: Conjuring the Sex Positive*. Berkeley, CA: ThreeL Media, 2017.

Solnit, Rebecca. *Hope in the Dark: Untold Histories, Wild Possibilities*. Chicago: Haymarket Books, 2016.

Solnit, Rebecca. *Men Explain Things to Me*. Chicago: Haymarket Books, 2015.

Taylor, Keeanga-Yamahtta. *From #Blacklivesmatter to Black Liberation*. Chicago: Haymarket Books, 2016.

Taylor, Keeanga-Yamahtta. *How We Get Free: Black Feminism and the Combahee River Collective*. Chicago: Haymarket Books, 2017.

Tovar, Virgie. *You Have the Right to Remain Fat*. New York: Feminist Press, 2018.

Traister, Rebecca. *All The Single Ladies*. New York: Simon & Schuster, 2016.

Traister, Rebecca. *Good and Mad: The Revolutionary Power of Women's Anger*. New York: Simon & Schuster, 2018.

Walker, Rebecca, ed. *To be real: Telling the truth and changing the face of feminism,* Anchor Books, 1995.

West, Lindy. *Shrill,* New York: Hachette, 2016.

West, Lindy. *The Witches are Coming,* New York, Hachette Books, 2019.

Zeisler, Andi. *We Were Feminists Once,* New York: Public Affairs, 2016.